MW00769244

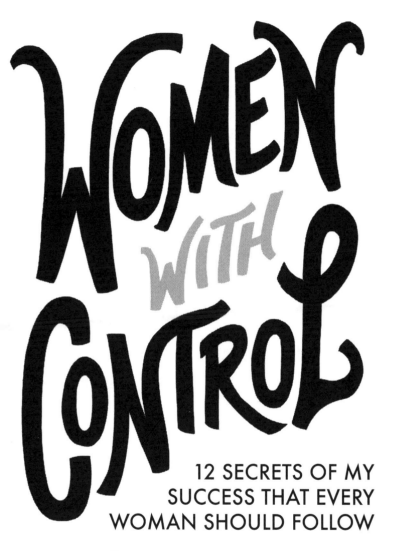

WOMEN WITH CONTROL

12 SECRETS OF MY SUCCESS THAT EVERY WOMAN SHOULD FOLLOW

RENÉE GREENSTEIN

© 2021 by Renee Greenstein. All Rights Reserved

Published by Simply Good Press, Montclair, New Jersey

http://www.simplygoodpress.com
Printed in the United States of America

All rights reserved. No part of this book may be reproduced by any mechanical, photographic, or electronic process, or in the form of a phonographic recording nor may it be stored in a retrieval system, transmitted, or otherwise copied for public or private use—other than for "fair use" as brief quotations embedded in articles and reviews— without prior written permission of the publisher.

For permissions requests, speaking inquiries, and bulk-order purchase options, visit www.ReneeGreenstein.com/book

Library of Congress Control Number: 2021900999

ISBN-13: print: 978-1-7352585-3-9
ISBN-13: eBook: 978-1-7352585-4-6

Cover Design: Maeve Norton
Interior Layout Design: Maeve Norton

I DEDICATE THIS BOOK TO:

Julius, my loving Dad who gave me the wings to fly.

Justin, my husband whose support and love gives me the strength to get through anything.

Corey, my heart.

Princess Aya and Master Levi, my grandchildren.

My Wardrobe Warriors who inspire me every day.

Women with Control

CHAPTER 1

Rule Their World

Well, hello there! I'm so happy you can join me, lovely lady, because we've got a LOT to talk about.

You know, I get it. You want to look good. <u>All. The. Time.</u> That's why you picked up this book. But let's get real. Sometimes, it's really hard to look your best. Life gets in the way of the perfectly styled hair or the gel manicure you couldn't fit into your schedule or your budget. Shirt buttons pop during a job interview. You get a run in your pantyhose on your way to a wedding. Your favorite silk skirt has a giant water stain and your cashmere sweater has moth holes. Game over.

Not so fast.

You may lose a round here or there — I know I do — but you are NOT out of the game. Not by a long shot.

You are so in it. In fact, let's be in it together. There's strength in numbers, right? And I know we can win if we put our minds to it. Because let's face it. We can get lost in the negativity that swirls in our heads, and we would be so much happier if we would only get out of our own way.

That's what being a Woman with Control is all about. Moving your way through life as if you own it. It doesn't matter if supposedly well-meaning friends push you to try the newest diet to shed the pounds you've recently gained. It doesn't matter if you get in a fender bender the day after purchasing that adorable red Mini Cooper. It doesn't matter if you've had a run of disastrous Tinder dates with guys who ditch and leave you with the bill.

You may have no control over the garbage life throws at you, but you can certainly control how you deal with the trash. Will you shower yourself off or leave the banana peel hanging in your hair?

I've been there. I *am* there. Sure, you may have seen me on QVC doing my No More Wiggle, No More Jiggle® dance, smiling and laughing away. That's because I genuinely love getting out there and talking about my fashion collections, Attitudes by Renee® and Women with Control®. I like seeing models of all sizes twirling around in my latest collections and seeing how great they look. It gives me great satisfaction to design clothes that flatter every woman's body with all their curves and variations.

But I have plenty of moments during the rest of my day when I'd like to take that squishy stress ball — the one I'm supposed to squeeze to relax — and shove it down the garbage disposal. I would take such pleasure in grinding it up into little bits.

Then I remind myself to take a breath. Inhale. Exhale. (I know you've heard this a thousand times, but trust me, it works.) Breathe in, breathe out. <u>Live your life with control.</u>

Women with Control understand that life can chew you up and spit you out. There's no success without pain, disappointment, people who try to sabotage you, and the endless grind of hard work.

If you get that and understand that it's all about how you maintain control over the garbage life throws at you, you will succeed at whatever it is you set your mind to. That is my promise to you if you decide you want to become a Woman with Control.

You're going to get to know me in this book, and I feel like I'm going to get to know you, too. So let's get acquainted, shall we? You can always contact me on any of my social media channels:

My website: ReneeGreenstein.com

Instagram: ReneeGreenstein_

Twitter: @rgreensteinqvc

Facebook: Renee Greenstein (@ReneeGreensteinQVC)

Facebook Group: Wardrobe Warriors

I read and respond to my messages and get into some great conversations with women who reach out to me. In fact, some of the Women with Control who appear in this book are those who reached out to me and were willing to share their transformational stories to help provide a little inspiration.

Women who buy my collections and let me know I've touched them in some way are the reason I am so committed to my craft. By buying and reading this book, you are also one of my inspirations. I am driven to design clothes that help women look and feel their best. That is the secret sauce to living your life with control — knowing that you are presenting your best self to the world.

Most important to me, though, is that you get to know yourself a little bit better as you turn the pages of this book — that you discover what's holding you back and how to move forward to a place of growth and fulfillment.

WE ALL HAVE THE FABULOUS IN US

Being a Woman with Control means looking like you own the world. You need to bring out the fabulous in you. We all have something special that's unique to our own brand of self. It might be your eyes, your walk, or your sparkling smile. You have a unique canvas, your own distinct features and body shape that make you who you are. But you can add things to that canvas to enhance it and turn it into a work of art.

You may not know yet which paints you want to put on that canvas, and that's perfectly fine. I'm inviting you on my journey to help you learn to identify the special inner and outer qualities of yourself that make you the special lady that you are. I'll help you get started painting on your canvas — or continuing the work of art that you've already begun. We'll dabble in some new colors and learn to take some style risks.

Give yourself permission to indulge and pamper yourself. You should be choosing styles, makeup, and accessories that put a smile on your face. You should be making yourself a priority, and that means setting aside a little time to focus on what you want to achieve and how you want to achieve it.

Looking your best is just one part of getting where you want to go, but it's an important part, and it's effort well spent because career success, romantic relationships, and even friendships all depend on the judgment someone forms when they first see you.

Think of how you are. You see someone for the first time and size them up, right? In fact, scientists say we all make snap decisions about a person's character, age, wealth, and likability within a few seconds of encountering someone new. Less than one-tenth of a second after seeing someone's face — well before that person says hello or extends her hand — we're judging their competence, according to a Princeton study. That's just the blink of an eye to make a good impression.

While beauty may be in the eye of the beholder, we know when we're looking fantastic, right? And when you know you look amazing, you feel more confident, more empowered, more like a Woman with Control.

Of course, there's the flip side, letting your appearance go could be a sign of depression. If you don't like yourself inside, you may not make much effort on the outside. We'll talk more about that later in this book.

ME IN A NUTSHELL

So who am I and why am I writing this book for you? What makes me the fashion maven? I'm a global fashion designer and founder of the Women with Control and Attitudes by Renee fashion lines, two of the best-selling fashion lines on QVC. You may have already bought some of my designs or heard one of my favorite mantras:

"Style is not about size; it's about attitude."

I say it again and again on my show. And I would say it to you if I met you on the street, whether on Fifth Avenue or in the Costco parking lot. I firmly believe that the more you feel free to accept yourself as you are, the more beautiful you will become. And I thoroughly enjoy dressing women like you, whether you're 18 or 80-plus years old.

My fashion and jewelry collections are headquartered in New York City, where I serve as President and Head Designer of my company, Two Chicks in the Backroom, Inc. I love, love, love Manhattan. It's a city that doesn't sleep, and as a person who gets by on four hours of sleep a night, I find that it offers me whatever I need at 1 a.m., whether it's a steak dinner, Alan Cummings at Joe's Pub, or Isaac Mizrahi's cabaret act at the Cafe Carlyle.

If I could sum up my mission in life, it would be: Create fashion lines to inspire women to express their true selves.

Clothes can help camouflage or display the varying personalities that we all have. We all have different sides of ourselves that we want to show at different times, depending on who we're with and what we're doing. I may dress more conservatively when I'm going to synagogue than when I'm heading out to dinner with my husband or going to a fashion show in Europe.

PHILOSOPHY OF LIFE/STYLE

I've been told I'm a strong woman. I know what I want, and I'm not afraid to make my wishes very clear to those around me. But people get that sense before I even open my mouth, just by looking at me, standing tall in clothes that flatter and accentuate my shape. Sure, I minimize my flaws with a little makeup, use jewelry and accessories to draw the eye to my best features, and wear only clothes that keep me comfortable and in control. But I also carry myself in a way that commands attention and tells the world I'm comfortable in my own skin. I'm proud of what I've got, and I'm getting better as the years go by.

My career has taken me to every corner of the world, affording me the opportunity to be with beautiful women from all different walks of life. Something we all have in common is that little bit of "attitude" that helps us stand out from the rest.

Like most little girls, I loved dressing up, and the prettier the outfit, the better. Even as a four-year-old, I had a knack for knowing my own style. I twirled about in my favorite pink dress with matching lace anklet socks. I knew how to work the room getting smiles from my father. One day, he rewarded me with his famous deep-dish blackberry pie. I gobbled it down and savored the sweet with the tart until l noticed the large purple stain that had spread on my favorite frilly dress. It was ruined, but I had learned an important lesson. After that, I was determined to look pristine and took extra precautions whenever I ate that pie. I loved looking at women dressed up in their heels and pillbox hats, and I knew that my hair ribbons needed to match my dress and that my dress needed to be free of blackberry stains.

Fast forward 15 years, and I decided to pursue a career in fashion in New York City. I wasn't tall — only about 5'6" — but I had long legs and was soon hired as a fit model — basically a human mannequin who helps designers drape, nip, and tuck their designs to determine the proper fit of their clothes. During my time as a fit model, I became aware that fashion catered to only a small group of women. And not real women with real bodies.

The clothes turned out to be made for actual mannequins, rather than the real women that we are.

But I also discovered my innate ability to communicate to designers and patternmakers how clothes fit and give suggestions on how clothing could be better made to fit all women. Over the years, I was inspired to create my own clothing lines, with sizes ranging from XXS to 3X and including petite and tall lengths, with the goal of empowering all women to look and feel their most beautiful.

I built my fashion line around a few mottos that I firmly believe in. As I already mentioned, "Style is not about size; it's about attitude" is my trademark phrase. Another one, which really defines my ultimate goal for my Women with Control collection, is "No More Wiggle, No More Jiggle."

Renee with Women with Control team member Jamie Ferry (left)

When strangers recognize me on the street, they run up to me and shout, "You're the No More Wiggle, No More Jiggle lady!" First I smile at them and say hello, and then I think, wow, am I glad I put on some lipstick and mascara before I ran out this morning.

So, what are some of your favorite mottos that get you through the day? It may seem a bit corny, but lining up a few sayings from people who inspire you can help you determine what you want most out of your look. Do you want to look fierce like Beyonce or mysterious like Marlene Dietrich? What words resonate with you when it comes to how you're feeling and what you aspire to be? We'll explore this more later, but here are some words that I find particularly inspiring from some of my favorite people.

"Our deepest fear is not that we are inadequate. Our deepest fear is that we are powerful beyond measure. It is our light, not our darkness that most frightens us. We ask ourselves, Who am I to be brilliant, gorgeous, talented, fabulous? Actually, who are you not to be? You are a child of God."

— NELSON MANDELA

"For me, every hour is grace. And I feel gratitude in my heart each time I can meet someone and look at his or her smile."

— ELI WIESEL

"A curve is the loveliest distance between two points."

— MAE WEST

"Don't not give 150%. The key is to really just give everything. Like, really, really give it all, so that you get back a ton. I think that's what the misunderstanding is. When you're younger, you just want to get, but you don't get unless you really put a lot into it."

— NORMA KAMALI

CHAPTER 2

Always look Fabulous — Even When Just Running Out To Buy Milk

This book is about looking your best to feel your best. It's about doing whatever it takes to feel empowered, so you can become a Woman with Control. I truly believe that when you look good and you feel good, no one can stop you from pursuing your dreams and making the difference you want to make in the world.

My bubbie — that's the Yiddish word for grandma — always gave me this bit of advice:

"Always look good, since you never know who you're going to meet."

It has served me well, because I've met people who recognize me from my QVC show around the world, on the streets of Manhattan, and at the Costco where I shop in King of Prussia, PA.

Even if you're not in the public eye, I'm sure you run into people you know in the most unexpected places. Or you may meet someone new while you're out doing errands or attending a school board meeting — perhaps even a potential job contact or romantic partner — and you may think to yourself:

I hope they didn't notice that my hair wasn't combed or that I had a stain on my blouse.

What a shame to leave a bad impression, especially when it doesn't take much to look put together — and not thrown together — at any time of the day. Being a Woman with Control means I take an extra 30 seconds before I head out the door to glance in the mirror, fix my lipstick, pat my hair, and make sure I don't have a stray piece of spinach stuck in my teeth.

My trademark is KISSS: Keep it smooth, simple, and sleek.

I've got a few tried and true pieces in my collection that never fail me. They're in perfect condition, they're wrinkle-free, and they fit me beautifully, hugging my curves in all the right places. Okay, I've got more than a few of these pieces. I keep adding as I create new designs for Women with Control or

Attitudes by Renee. But you really just need a few truly "best friend" items of clothing that will never let you down.

Black leggings, dark pants, and a few A-line skirts or dresses in neutral colors (black, brown, or gray).

Once you've got your bottom half set, choose a top that pops with color, cut, or an interesting pattern. If you don't have time to do a full makeup routine, just grab lipstick or lip gloss to smooth a little color on your lips and you're done.

Another one of my mottos is that the right shade of lipstick will always enhance your look and give you a little boost, even if you're not feeling particularly fashionable that day. And it only takes about three seconds to apply. If it's your first time wearing lipstick, go to the makeup counter at a department store to get a few shades recommended for you.

"I used to be a fashion don't," says Patrice Blaszkowski, a 62-year-old teacher and grandmother from Bethlehem, PA.

Patrice told me she never had to think about fashion in her younger years. "I wore a Catholic school uniform for 12 years, so I never really had to think much about what to wear through high school," she explains. Years of raising three kids and working full time as a junior high school teacher left her with little time to think about fashion. "I was never good at picking outfits for myself. I only wore baggy LL Bean dresses and khakis and polo shirts. Finally I got to the point where I thought 'I'm too old for this. I need to get something that looks better on me.'"

She decided to purchase a few items from my collection in 2017, trying out the black slacks and leggings with 14% butt-lifting spandex, and says she felt transformed. "I feel much more confident because I know I look good, and I get such positive feedback on how I dress," she says. "I teach at a school for budding artists and they do pay attention, and for the first time in my career, they're complimenting me and asking about my tunic or the bangle bracelets I use to accessorize."

Her biggest gain? She now has more time in the morning, because everything mixes and matches. And she doesn't need to pack gym clothes; the pants are comfortable enough for her to slip on some sneakers and do her walking routine at lunch.

"I feel sexier when I go out; my husband notices my curves, and I just know I'm looking my best. Now I think I'm a fashion do, absolutely."

Patrice Balszkowski, Wardrobe Warrior

WHY LOOKING GOOD HELPS
YOU FEEL GOOD

I probably don't need to tell you that how you dress — the style, cut, and color of the clothes you choose to wear — reflects an important part of your identity and how you wish the world to see you. But you may not realize that the act of putting on a particular outfit can actually transform how you think about yourself. Research suggests that certain clothing choices can instill the belief that you are a Woman with Control, ruler of your own world. And this can actually help you perform and think better. Scientists call this "enclothed cognition," and Northwestern University researchers designed a clever study to prove that "dress for success" is a real phenomenon.

Volunteers in the study were asked to answer questions to test their attention to detail while wearing a scientist's lab coat, a painter's smock, or their own clothes. Participants performed much better on the tests when wearing the lab coat than when they were dressed as a painter or in their own clothes. (The same volunteers reported that a lab coat is generally associated with attentiveness and carefulness in a pretest administered by the researchers.)

"Although the saying goes that clothes do not make the man," the researchers concluded, "our results suggest they do hold a strange power over their wearers."

I would argue that it's not a strange power at all. We take on different personas based on our outfits of choice. When I'm taking a power walk in my sneakers and leggings, I feel like a can-do, elite athlete. And I feel and act sexier when I'm wearing my favorite black cocktail dress that shows off my legs and flatters my curves. I'm sure you feel it too when you're showing off a little cleavage or applying a bold red lipstick.

But once you button up a blazer and slip on the heels, you probably feel and act like a power player, walking with a straight back and determined strides rather than in the slinky slither of a cocktail dress. You wear it. You own it. You become it.

Think of Diana Prince. She knew she needed her killer Wonder Woman costume if she was going to kick Lex Luthor's butt.

British psychologist Karen Pine writes in *Mind What You Wear* that clothing has huge transformational power and that the act of buying a simple stunning hat has the potential to set off a whole chain of events that can change how you see yourself. When you put on a purple leather jacket or hide your straight brown hair under a curly blond wig, you may see yourself in a completely new way. You may even give yourself permission to behave differently. Maybe you're more outgoing, positive, confident. Maybe you want to bring out your inner tough girl for the night. "One small item, a twist of tailoring, a splash of color, a wardrobe tweak, can alter how we think, feel and behave," Pine writes.

Of course, you don't need a daring accessory to be and act fabulous. But what if there are facets of yourself that you haven't yet explored? Or what if you just want to reach a little further or a little higher? Can your clothing choices actually help you do that?

As part of her research into fashion psychology, Pine conducted a study that found that college students feel more assured of their own ability to get things done when they're wearing a superhero t-shirt. Diana Prince was definitely onto something with the Wonder Woman bodice and golden tiara!

I'm so convinced of clothing's power to transform our beliefs about ourselves that I have a new collection of self-affirmation t-shirts expressing certain truths that I think we should all live by.

Mirror mirror on the wall, age doesn't matter after all.

Life's not a dress rehearsal; live for today.

LOOKING YOUR BEST WHILE
WORKING AT HOME

When the coronavirus pandemic hit the U.S. in March, we entered a new reality – one that kept nearly the entire nation pretty much homebound. We worked from home, went to yoga classes from home, had family reunions with everyone zooming in from their home, and hosted holiday celebrations on Facetime. Like others on TV, I did my QVC show from my living room in Pennsylvania. It was an incredible challenge, and one I would like never to repeat.

As I write this section of the chapter, Americans are still stuck in their homes. Many of us have been wearing the same yoga pants day after day. Sure, we may swipe one t-shirt for another or don a hoodie on chilly days, but is this really the time to think about fashion?

"We dress to tell a story about ourselves and if there is no one there to hear our narrative, we've been put on mute — turned into mere ectoplasm in pajamas," wrote Washington Post fashion critic Robin Givhan in a column posted in March.

But, she argues, we should not allow ourselves to become these ectoplasms. We need to take advantage of even those small moments when we leave our homes to, say, take the dog for a walk or grab a gallon of milk from the neighborhood store.

"Our clothes can be our pep talk, an impassioned soliloquy, Givhan wrote. "As we scurry along the street, dutiful in our social distancing, our clothes become glancing waves —

reminders that at some point we will speak to each other again."

I would argue that being stuck in my home reminded me that I'm really not dressing for others, I'm dressing for myself. All those countless hours spent in my house left me more time to look in the mirror. And every time I looked in the mirror, I felt a little ping of happiness when I looked like my best self. I also felt a little down or grumpy when I gazed at a reflection that showed I hadn't made my best effort to put myself together.

Renee working at home during the Covid-19 pandemic

We all got a glimpse of this during those countless Zoom conference calls. Which family members, friends or coworkers kept their cameras turned off? Likely they were the ones who just couldn't bring themselves to be more than ectoplasm in pajamas.

Every time, I gaze at myself in my bathroom mirror, I feel a little pick-me-up when I look like my usual put-together self. Okay, I may not be wearing heels and a silk blazer but my comfortable casual wear by Women with Control or Attitudes by Renee help me put forward my best look even while lounging in my house.

It may seem counterintuitive but I firmly believe that when you're stuck in your home, that's exactly the time you need to make an effort to look your best. You need to value your own self-assessment, not just the assessment of others. If you look in the mirror and like what you see, you will definitely get a mood boost. So, take that shower, shave your legs, wash your hair, and put on a little lipstick. All of these self-care measures can be a great form of therapy.

You think no one will see you, but you have a lot of time to see yourself. When we spend our days running errands, going to work and doing carpools, we often don't have time to contemplate how we look. It's the time we spend under stay-at-home orders that we realize how important it is to <u>make an effort</u>.

OTHER WAYS TO BOOST YOUR CONFIDENCE

Beyond clothes, there are a host of other external things that can boost your confidence. In 2014, car manufacturer Kia took a survey of what makes people feel confident. I was interested to see what topped the list for women:

Top 20 Things That Make a Woman feel Confident

1. A new haircut
2. A sunny day
3. Walking in heels
4. Learning a new skill

5. Booking a vacation ✓

6. Shaved legs

7. Lipstick

8. Glowing tan ✓

9. Little black dress ✓

10. Designer perfume ✓

11. A day off ✓

12. Being asked out on a date

13. Matching lingerie

14. Eating a healthy breakfast ✓

15. Going to the gym ✓

16. Diamond ring

17. A blow-dry ✓

18. Whitened teeth ✓

19. Chatting with a friend or close relative

20. Pant suit

Men reported that they felt more confident with, among other things, a freshly shaved face, new suit, and brushed teeth.

To me, feeling strong and empowered comes with feeling competent and in control. Of course, you can't control everything in your world. Illness, accidents, and financial turmoil can all come unexpectedly through no fault of your own. (I've seen my share of crises throughout my life.)

But feeling a sense of mastery over what you <u>can</u> control is the ultimate path to confidence. When it comes to your own personal style, I firmly believe that keeping it simple, sleek, and easy is the key to boosting your confidence in how you look and feel. I design my collections with that idea in mind.

Renee's 7 Fashion Collection Commandments

1. Clothes should never make you feel ashamed, even if you've gained a few pounds.

2. Pants and dresses should be easy to pull on and slip into.

3. An outfit should flatter (not detract from) your figure.

4. Style should be ageless. My clothes are appropriate for any age — whether you're 21 or 101.

5. A collection should be height appropriate, cut to fit a woman who's 4'10" just as well as someone who's 5'11".

6. Weight should not be an excluding factor; clothing should be made to fit all body sizes. (Don't get me started on body-shaming fashion lines that don't have any sizes above a 10.)

7. A woman should feel better about herself and her body after putting on one of my pieces because the clothes should be designed to bring out the best in you, to make you feel comfortable and help you feel confident.

Bottom line: You should feel good about the clothes you wear and how you look in them. It's my job to design collections that will make you feel this way.

DESIGNERS WHO INSPIRE ME

I'm proud to say I stand on the shoulders of fashion giants who came before me. Two of my favorite giants? Donna Karan and Norma Kamali. Karan came up with the concept of "Seven Easy Pieces" based on the idea that assembling a few smart basics was the key to good style. As she told a reporter in 1985 when she launched her first collection, "So many women find assembling the right clothes bewildering today. They've discovered fast ways to put food on the table, but they do not know how to get their wardrobes together easily."

Her seven basics included a bodysuit, a pair of tights, a versatile skirt, a pair of loose slacks, a tailored jacket, a cashmere sweater, and a classic white shirt. Of course, she added to those over the years: a large scarf that could be worn as a wrap skirt, shawl, or knotted neck piece became a mainstay, as did a black leather jacket and the LBD (little black dress).

Karan's overall philosophy was to give all women access to a chic wardrobe. She was inclusive, designing seven easy pieces that could work for any body type. And she understood that comfort was tantamount.

Kamali, inventor of the sleeping bag coat, made fleece and denim into high fashion, and she kicked off the trend of athlete-inspired lifestyle clothes. She's passionate about self-care and looking good to feel good. In one of her blog posts, she recounts how she completely let herself go when she was first starting her fashion business:

"Here's what the early of years of running my own business looked like: It's been too long since I shaved my legs or armpits. My hair is a frazzled mess, and I'm basically wearing a uniform every day. I haven't been eating real meals, there's no time to see friends, and my refrigerator has ancient condiments and things too old to eat. In short, I let my self-care fall by the wayside."

She realized she needed to take better care of herself after catching her reflection in the mirror at her design studio and shuddering at the "scary sight." She determined to put herself on her to-do list and began getting more sleep, reducing her caffeine intake, and keeping her hair freshly cut and styled.

That realization led Kamali on a path to creating designs that would help women feel good about themselves.

"As a designer," Kamali observes in her book *Facing East: Ancient Health and Beauty Secrets for the Modern Age*, "I've seen how easy it is for women to feel not thin enough or not pretty enough. I've watched women let a bad hair day or an inability to fit into a skirt be powerful enough to take them down. It's cultural sabotage that begins early in life, but it's also self-inflicted."

What do you want the world to see when you fly out of your house in the morning and greet the world? Who do you want to uplift in your interactions? What kind of an impact do you want to have on the world?

When you begin to think of your life as a meaningful enterprise, you will be joining me on that mission. Looking good, feeling good, and doing good should go hand in hand. So let's join hands, shall we?

CHAPTER 3

Draw on Their Inner Strength and Beauty

I design clothes for real women. I'm inspired by them. I empathize with them. I AM one of them. I can be sitting alongside a runway during New York fashion week, wearing my Women with Control knit pants and a top by the designer of the show — and I know I look great. But I also still feel like myself. I'm keenly aware that I'm not a famous actress like the woman sitting to my right or the supermodel turned reality show star sitting to my left. Like all women, I sometimes question whether I truly belong with the "successful" folks that I'm sitting with.

Many women have these misgivings. We may have imposter syndrome, feeling like frauds from time to time, especially when we've reached an important point of success. Is this fancy house really mine? Did I really earn that job promotion? Can I really be the mother of this beautiful baby? But then we have to remind ourselves that we deserve life's blessings, and I truly believe in counting them. My granddaughter Aya, my grandson Levi, my husband Justin, and my son Corey are my biggest blessings.

We also need to acknowledge that we're a product of our upbringing and that we will often carry baggage from our childhood and how our parents raised us.

My father poured his unconditional love all over me, bathing me in it, making me feel good about myself. My dad was my life. He was both my mother and my father. He was a chef, and he taught me the pleasure of savoring food, a love of fashion, and how to be a kind, caring, compassionate person. He called me his bumble bee and told me I was born almost as if announcing myself to the world, HERE I AM. I didn't want to miss a thing, and I wanted the world to sit up and take notice and see what I could do.

My mother, well, let's just say I refer to her as "the woman who gave birth to me," and leave it at that.

Renee, age 13, with her father Julius Nathaniel McKnight

As a black Jewish woman starting a business, I had to prove myself. When I walked into synagogue late on a Shabbat morning, people noticed. I couldn't hide. It was obvious I was the girl who stood out.

I was raised by my Dad and didn't really have my mother's influence in my life. That was fine with me. I learned to use my ability to overcome fear and discomfort to my advantage, especially the business world.

I was on a job interview many years ago, and the man interviewing me said, "For a broad, you want a lot of money." I looked him in the eye and replied, "Yes, I do." I got the job at the salary I demanded.

I don't have a college education; I dropped out during my freshman year. But I learned from my own resilience and how my father brought me up that I can do things. With that inner strength, I was able to establish a brand and sell it.

I also knew that I'd need to never let them see me sweat. While I'm not plagued with sweat stains when I'm anxious, I know many women are, and I know they need a garment that will keep them from revealing their anxiety in high-pressure situations. Few of us want to wear our emotions on our sleeves – I mean literally. We need to know our clothes won't throw us under the bus when we're giving that power-point presentation to our boss's boss or making a toast at our best friend's wedding.

For this reason, I decided to create a moisture-wicking garment that would prevent sweat stains. My fashion pieces are steadfast and true and will not reveal what you don't want them to reveal!

GETTING STARTED

How did I get from an awkward 13-year-old to a fashion model in the fur industry by the time I was in my late teens? I wouldn't have believed it myself if you had told me before it happened. I'm 5'6½", far too short to be a model. I was raised as a very proper girl, not one who would spend all day wearing nothing but a little teddy under a long fur coat. But that's exactly what I did after a friend connected me to a furrier looking for a showroom model in Manhattan's garment district.

My assets were my long legs. They gave me the appearance of height and made me look statuesque. I still love my legs, but now I also appreciate what they do for me. They enable me to dance to my heart's content, propel me from place to place, gliding, walking, running through life.

Don't get me wrong. Modeling furs had its challenges. Wearing a coat all day through the summer months in a showroom that wasn't air conditioned was brutal. So were the male buyers who asked to look at the coat's lining while I was wearing it, just so they could get a better look at my lingerie-clad body. (I learned to run into the back room and quickly change into another coat to show them the lining of the coat that I previously had on.)

I also learned that I had a knack for selling. I wasn't a mannequin wearing a coat, but a capable young woman who learned quickly. I could describe the differences in pelt quality, country of origin, and benefits of cropped vs. full-skin cuts. I was a showroom model, but I knew whatever I put on, the buyers would order.

That gave me confidence. Confidence to start running a showroom and eventually to start my own fashion line.

But there were bumps, many of them, along the way — big ones that tripped me up, smacked me down, and made me never want to lift myself off the ground ever again.

One of those bumps was an eating disorder that I developed shortly after my son Corey was born. I was 18, newly married, and just starting my career as a model when I became pregnant. After I gave birth, I had a sinking feeling that I was done, kaput, finished. My waistline would never be the same. Pregnancy had done me in. I had an inner voice in my head, chastising me, telling me I was too fat and no good. So I stopped eating and then binged and purged. My weight dropped to 90 pounds, and I was hospitalized for anorexia and bulimia.

I don't remember what compelled me to survive. I wanted to live for my son and for my amazing first husband Doug, who was the passionate force that drove me to my early successes. (He died tragically young from cancer, which was perhaps the biggest hurdle I've ever had to face, but I'll tell you more about that later.)

Somewhere deep down, I knew I needed to rise from the ashes to try to make something of myself. How could I quit before I'd even gotten started? Somewhere inside me was another inner voice, fighting the one telling me I was fat and worthless. This voice warned me that I'd be a total loser if I gave into my fears and gave up. This voice told me I was born to fight and kick the hell out of my inner demons.

IMPORTANCE OF
EMPOWERING YOURSELF

While we didn't speak about "empowerment" much in those days, I was really seeking a way to empower myself — even if I didn't have the word for it — and live my best life. I knew deep down that I was a beautiful person who could have a real impact on the world in my own way. And I firmly believe that all women have this inner strength. They just need to tap into it. We need to teach children to tap into it too.

It's a message I try to convey to my little princess, Aya. My granddaughter is 14, and I hope she smiles when she reads this part about her. I also hope she believes me when I tell her, "You can do anything you want to do if you really go for it."

Renee and her granddaughter Aya

Aya, honey, you'd better be willing to work hard and to take the punches life throws your way because, little lady, there will be punches — some pretty hard ones — that you're gonna need to rise from even if you're knocked flat on your face!

Of course, I want to convey these same messages to my little prince, Levi, who is five years old. I want him to be strong and proud of his identity as a Jewish man of color. I also want him to be respectful and supportive of any future romantic partner he has — way, way down the road.

I'm continually inspired by women who get knocked down and get back up. They have the Rocky spirit in them. As a wise woman named Jenette Stanley once said: "Don't be the girl who fell. Be the girl who got back up."

One of my inspirations is Donna Cashman, a 63-year-old twice-divorced mother of three who describes her life as "not an easy one" — which is like saying Warren Buffett is a bit wealthy. Donna says she was in an abusive marriage and caring for her adult daughter with special needs when she lost her job of 22 years. When the factory closed down four years ago, Donna was told she might not get any severance for being laid off and that her pension was in jeopardy. She was potentially facing homelessness while in the middle of a nasty divorce, with legal bills piling up. "Through much prayer and determination and God's grace, I was blessed with a new job caring for the elderly as a concierge in an assisted living facility," Donna told me in a Facebook message.

After two decades of wearing a factory uniform, she was faced with having to dress professionally, though in a kind of uniform of sorts, black pants and a white shirt. "I was 5'10" and weighed only 119 pounds, and any pants I bought kept falling down on me especially once I tucked the work-issued walkie-talkie into my waistband." She caught one of my shows on QVC and bought a pair of XXS leggings. When she tried them on, a light bulb went off.

"I slipped on the leggings and looked fabulous. These pants made me feel so confident; everyone has this idea that the skinnier you are the better, but I also had a real problem I was struggling with, and until I put these leggings on, I was convinced I would never find a pair of pants that fit and flattered my figure. I have been trying my whole life to gain weight and always felt too emaciated and sickly looking. My butt was totally flat until I put on these pants and got a lift. Gravity hits everyone with age, and these clothes reversed that."

Donna Cashman, Wardrobe Warrior

While I'm thrilled that Donna got such an emotional lift from my clothes, I find her story inspiring because of her resilience. She is the ultimate woman with control. Once she started dressing in clothes that made her feel beautiful, she felt transformed. "I wore an Attitudes by Renee top with a cape attached to it to work and felt like Super Woman. If you're gonna wear a cape, you'd better act like a superhero. I was brought up to be your best, look your best, and act your best, and that's what I did. I was often the first contact visiting friends and family made when they walked in the door, and I knew I needed to represent my employer well."

BUILDING RESLIENCE

There are loads of best-selling books about building resilience, and I'm not going to delve into them here. In a nutshell, psychologists think of resilience as something that a lucky few are born with — a natural optimistic attitude that allows us to bounce back from life's challenges. But these experts also believe that resilience can be cultivated and grown, like a muscle, if we practice smart techniques. One of these techniques is adopting a "growth mindset" rather than a "fixed mindset."

Having a fixed mindset means you're likely to avoid challenges, give up easily, and ignore useful negative feedback. Having a growth mindset means you're likely to take on challenges, persevere when times get tough, and learn from criticism so you can change what you're doing wrong to make yourself more successful.

You don't need to guess which mindset leads to more resilience. (Hint: It begins with a G.)

What fascinates me, though, is the intersection of style and resilience. There are actually certain hairstyles, clothing choices, and makeup moves we can use to build our inner strength when times are tough. We can make certain style choices to protect ourselves from going down a slippery slope when the world is crashing down.

Think about it. What drove Donna to completely revamp her style when she had more important things on her mind, like impending divorce and the possibility of foreclosure?

Part of it is survival mode, a drive to push ourselves to the surface when we're drowning.

But I think part of it is that we have, deep down, the inner knowledge that crisis often comes with growth.

And sometimes we just need a change just to get out of a rut.

In a blog post titled "Why Changing Your Style And Spinning Into An Identity Crisis Are Actually Awesome Things," fashion blogger Marlen Komar admits that changing your style can be a scary thing. But she also points out that "feeling your style move in a completely new direction is exciting because it means something inside you shifted along the way while you weren't looking. You've grown, even if you weren't ready for it. *Especially* if you weren't ready for it."

I love this because I think we all get bored with our clothes, our hair, our makeup. And we do need to mix things up a bit, take some risks. It shows that we're adventurous and that we're comfortable enough in our own skin to try something new. That's why I dyed my hair blond. I knew NO ONE would think it was my natural color, and in a way, it was me declaring to the world that I am not afraid of going against nature's choices for me.

This is all part of having a growth mindset. It's part of being resilient. Voila! I found that intersection of style and resilience after all. (Bet you didn't think I would!)

CHAPTER 4

Know How To Use Makeup To Their Advantage

Here's my take on makeup. Yes, it's a must. But less is definitely more.

End of chapter. (Just kidding.)

I firmly believe that Women with Control know that they can benefit from a little fine tuning, whether it's applying blush to their cheekbones, mascara to their lashes, or a dash of color to their lips. The goal is not to camouflage yourself; it's to enhance your looks to bring out your full beautiful potential.

To me, makeup is an accessory that, like a well-tied scarf, perfectly positioned belt, or bold statement necklace, can complete an outfit and make you look more polished.

But I control my makeup; I don't let it control me. That means I don't spend a lot of time putting it on — maybe 10 minutes max. I'm not looking to paint the Mona Lisa every morning — just give my look a little boost. So I never leave my house without a little eyeliner applied to my upper eyelids, some moisturizing foundation smoothed on my face, a touch of mascara, and a fresh application of lipstick.

For an evening out, I'll take a little more time to create a more dramatic face. I'm a big fan of magnetic eyelash enhancers. (I can never apply the glue correctly on false eyelashes, and these don't have glue.) I'll also add a bolder shade of lipstick (dark brown or red) and use blush to create contoured cheekbones. I spend more time on makeup when I get ready to go on camera for QVC, but the stylists know not to put heavy makeup on me. I like the most natural look I can get.

This may all sound complicated, but it's really not. And quite frankly, you don't need to follow my lead. Do what makes you feel like you're putting your best face forward.

If you feel like you're all thumbs with makeup, I recommend going to the makeup counter at a good department store and asking a sales person to help you pick out a basic eyeshadow, liner, lipstick, blush, and foundation. They routinely throw in a free lesson on how to apply them. Make sure to emphasize your overall philosophy. Are you going for a natural look? Do you need a more formal look for an upcoming wedding? What are your best features that you want to make pop?

THE MAKEUP-FREE TREND

But why make yourself up at all? Why should you when some of our favorite stars are baring it all with nude faces on magazine covers?

Demi Lovato, Gisele Bündchen, and Alicia Vikander all went makeup free for their Vogue covers. So did Christina Aguilera for Paper magazine, saying, "I'm at the place, even musically, where it's a liberating feeling to be able to strip it all back and appreciate who you are and your raw beauty." Alicia Keys had her revolution (or revolt) against makeup in 2016, when she pledged to no longer wear makeup in public as "part of her journey toward self-empowerment." (As far as I can see, she's still maintaining that stance.)

While I applaud these women for taking a stand and appreciating their natural beauty, I don't think women need to throw out their cosmetic bags to feel strong and empowered. We should not be made to feel guilty or ashamed for wanting to enhance our beauty.

But if you want to go bare faced, go right ahead and own your style!

If you do wear makeup — which is my personal preference — do a quick self-assessment and determine what you need to look your best without using perfection as your goal. You don't need to look perfect. (No one does!) And you certainly shouldn't skip experiences in the quest to always look your best. Some of us get so caught up in looking perfect and primed all the time that we skip the gorgeous hike in the national park or avoid diving through a wave in the ocean.

If you're among those who feel this way, then it may be a good idea to take a makeup-free day and live a little in your own natural look. You should not be missing out on fun in an effort to look flawless! In fact, sometimes not wearing makeup makes you look younger.

I posted on Facebook a while ago that I did a makeup-free day, and I found it profoundly empowering. Now I do it every so often. It's all about feeling good about yourself and owning it.

Okay, now that I've got that off my chest, let's consider the upsides of eyeshadow and blush.

Beauty executive Laura Geller, whom I admire greatly, has a phenomenally successful cosmetic line that she's been selling on QVC for more than two decades. Her products are wonderful, but I think her biggest selling point is that she understands how to demystify the use of makeup and provide women with tips on achieving what she calls "approachable beauty." She understands that applying makeup can be intimidating for many women who are afraid of messing up, applying too-bright eyeshadow, obviously penciled-in eyebrows, or runny mascara.

After all, we really don't want people to notice our makeup, just how beautiful we look. Right?

Geller gets that. In an interview with Forbes magazine, she says, "It's about taking away the mystification of and the daunting task of makeup, which a lot of women, even sophisticated women, felt threatened by. If you gave someone a million things to do on their face, they'd end up using probably two or three of them."

You can get some great makeup application tips from her on her website: laurageller.com.

Her personal beauty philosophy is that "makeup is every woman's birthright" and that putting your makeup on should be a joyous time of your day.

It sounds a little corny, I know. Really? I should feel joy putting on makeup?

But think about it. Your face is your canvas, and you are adding color and shading to transform it into a beautiful painting. The next time you put on lipstick, really look at what a difference a little color makes. When you sweep on your mascara or eyeliner, look at how much larger and more expressive your eyes look.

Once you feel these little lifts in your mood, that small surge of pleasure, you'll understand what she means by "joyous time of your day."

And again, less is more with your makeup. You don't need to go to heavy on the color. Hold back and be strategic about adding a pop of color to accentuate a certain feature. I'm always amazed at how adding a bright lipstick or smoky eye for evening can change my whole outlook.

GETTING A SKINCARE ROUTINE

Whether you choose to wear makeup or not, I ask only that you don't neglect your skin. While makeup can cover up blemishes and other skin flaws, I spend more time trying to keep my skin in good shape to keep my face in optimal condition. There are a few skin care routines you should absolutely adopt if you want to ensure that your skin ages well.

My routine is très simple. I just cleanse my face, pat on a toner, and apply some moisturizer (making sure not to forget my neck). In the morning, I use a gentle non-soap cleanser and take 10 seconds to dab on the toner. The real time saver comes from using tinted moisturizer. It serves double duty to moisturize and even my skin tone so I don't need foundation. At night, I repeat, using a non-tinted moisturizer. There, finished.

Oops! Do not forget your lips! I use a thin coating of Vaseline on mine before I apply lipstick in the morning.

Sunscreen is also a must. Many daily moisturizers contain sunscreens with SPF 15 or higher, which can be a convenient time saver.

In the evening, I make sure to remove all my makeup. (I never go to sleep with any on — it's a huge no-no.) I apply a heavier moisturizer at night and twice a week, I use a Clarisonics device --developed by Dr. Rob on QVC-- along with a special mixture cleanser that I developed to cleanse my face.

Again, your bare skin is your canvas, and you need to take good care of it before you even think about applying makeup.

The same holds true for your hair. Your hair will likely change as you age. It may thin out or change to a coarser texture as the melanin diminishes and the gray sets in. You may find that you look better with a slightly lighter hair color as you age. I've evolved from a natural brunette to a honey blonde. Dark hair just no longer works for me. My blond hair brightens my complexion, hiding the sallow tones that we all begin to develop after age 40.

I know that immediately after I get my hair colored, I can see an instant transformation in my complexion. I look like I'm glowing again. I also admire women who embrace their gray, letting their silver streaks or full silver mane shine through. Realize, though, that this, too, may require professional help to achieve a luminous color.

While I'm not an avid user of supplements, I have found that taking one with biotin has worked well for me in helping to keep my hair, nails, and skin healthy. I also take a daily multi-vitamin just to cover my nutritional bases on days when I'm not quite getting enough fruits, vegetables, and whole grains. This works for me, but I recommend checking with your doctor before taking any supplements to make sure they will not interfere with any health issues or medications you may be taking.

My secret sauce is hot water with lemon and fresh ginger root. It's usually the last thing I have in the evening and the first thing I have in the morning. It's an essential part of my wind down (and wake up) ritual and makes me feel healthier. I highly recommend it.

A WORD ON PLASTIC SURGERY

Okay here's my reveal: I haven't used Botox or injectable fillers yet to keep my skin smooth and my wrinkles minimized. I can probably thank the good genes I inherited from my parents and grandparents. But that doesn't mean I'm opposed to using these modern-day miracles the minute I see things falling apart. I believe in aging gracefully — and yes, with control — which in my opinion, doesn't mean you need to embrace every wrinkle and age spot.

Excuse me, but your house needs remodeling every once in a while, so what's wrong with feeling like you need to give yourself an update? I'm not against it if you do it for yourself and not for anyone else. I'm also very supportive of women who are adamantly opposed to plastic surgery or dermatology treatments. You should do what feels true to you.

Now I'm holding up a flashing yellow light. Proceed with caution! Some women may be tempted to go overboard on plastic surgery, way beyond the tweaking and fine tuning. They want to do a total overhaul, like tearing a house down and building a new one from scratch. I know I used the house analogy already, but I can tell you that the comparison ends there. You are not a fixer-upper that requires a total renovation. **Do not let anyone tell you otherwise.**

With that in mind, beware of any doctor who takes a photo, circles all your imperfections, and tells you how they can be fixed — like those featured on the extreme surgery reality shows. If you see a doctor like that, run! We've all seen celebrity plastic surgery disasters. Faces of stars we once loved are now unrecognizable.

Think of it as updating your hair style. You don't bring a photo of Jennifer Aniston to your stylist and say, make me look like her. You ask if that cut will work with the shape of your face and your hair. Well, the same goes for that nose, lips, or tush that you envy. You might be able to get some tweaks to alter that one feature, but you won't look like the movie star afterward. And why should you?

Women with Control want to look like themselves — only better.

OWNING THE GLAM

Consider this a public service announcement for embracing your glamorous side. Being a Woman with Control means getting yourself glamorous on a regular basis. Not once a year on New Year's Eve or for a family wedding. I'd say at least once a month. Better yet, once a week!

Makeup artist to the stars Mally Roncal articulates the importance of glam beautifully. Mally, whom I know and adore from her QVC show and makeup line, says her mother was the original inspiration for her love of beauty and glamour. "She was a doctor and she was always done. Like hair, makeup, heels, nail, clothes, Chanel, the whole thing. She was very particular and I literally remember sitting at her boudoir with her and watching her do her face and she would sort of teach me as she was going along," Mally said in an interview with Glamour magazine. When Mally was just 17, her mother died of breast cancer, and she drew on her mother's credo — "looking good makes people feel good" — to develop her makeup line.

Every woman deserves to look as gorgeous on the outside as she feels on the inside, Mally says, not just the Hollywood A-listers.

One of the secrets of Mally's success was that, as a Filipino-American, she understood that women of color should feel empowered to celebrate the differences that make them unique, fierce, and fabulous. They should not be erasing their ethnic differences, but enhancing them. It's no wonder Rihanna, Beyonce, Angelina Jolie, Jennifer Lopez, and Heidi Klum have all hired Mally as a makeup artist.

CHAPTER 5

Wear Colors and Cuts That Work for Them

Style is not about size; it's about attitude. So how does a Woman with Control dress with *attitude*?

How should you put together an outfit that tells the world, "This is who I am"?

Every woman is unique, so how I dress with attitude may be completely different from how you dress with attitude. And that's wonderful. You want your style to reveal an essential part of your identity as well as your personality. It should reflect your best YOU.

A Woman with Control also understands that she doesn't need to be a slave to her style. If you always wear a black cocktail dress to formal weddings, why can't you switch it up every once in a while by donning a gold sequined dress and purple stilettos? Maybe you're just looking to let your inner party girl out for the night. Or maybe you want to blend in with the crowd, so you decide to forgo your usual bright wardrobe for a little black dress: simple, sophisticated, and safe.

As I discussed in Chapter 2, dressing a certain way can give you a feeling of power or change aspects of your personality to make you feel more confident and in control.

There is no one "right" way to dress. Women with Control understand that and adopt the attitude of putting on clothes that make them feel good and reflect the mood they want to be in. Let's call it "aspirational dressing," or dressing to transform your attitude.

My philosophy is to design clothes that flatter women of all shapes and sizes. As I mentioned earlier, I had the vision to create my fashion collection to adjust to my own changing body with clothes that would smooth out the wiggles and jiggles. My Women with Control pants would hug women in all the right places to accentuate and lift — and minimize common problem areas like our tummies, back of thighs, and love handles around the waist. I wanted tunics and dresses that were more fitted in the chest and semi-fitted through the waist and hips that draped naturally to provide a smooth curve, while also providing some coverage.

My personal belief is that you can never have too many black leggings and pants. But I also encourage you to experiment with a pant or legging color that pops. Step out of your comfort zone! Try the burgundy leggings or the crop pants in jade green. Pair them with a printed top that has the same color as an accent or with a solid top in the same color for a monochromatic look. Sure, you can never go wrong with blacks and grays, but we all need a little color in our lives, especially during dreary winter months.

CHOOSING COLORS THAT WORK FOR YOU

You may think you know what styles, colors, and cuts work best for you. But I think most women can benefit from a brief "style 101". Here's a quick and dirty review of some smart fashion rules of thumb for getting clothes that flatter you most.

Black, of course, flatters and slenderizes nearly all of us, which is why we fill our closets with it.

But look beyond the black and take an accounting of what colors you see in your closet. You probably have clothes in similar shades like earth tones (brown, taupe, olive) or jewel tones (emerald green, purple, ruby red). You likely already have a sense of which colors look better on you because of your skin tone.

If you're not sure which colors work for you, you'll need to identify your skin tone. That can be a bit tricky. First, you want to determine whether you've got a cool or a warm undertone.

The FashionSpot website recommends turning your hand palm up and taking a look at the underside of your wrist to examine the color of your veins. If they're blue or purple, you're cool toned. It they look like they have a green or yellowish cast, you're warm toned.

Most women are **dark cools**, meaning they have a blue undertone in their skin. Another way to tell is to look at your natural hair color. If you have black or dark to medium brown hair with no reddish or orange undertones, you're probably a dark cool.

Dark cool tones can have a range of skin colors from fair to olive to tan to dark brown.

The most flattering colors for dark cools include: black

and white, royal blue, deep purple, fuchsia, emerald green, turquoise, and carnation red.

If you have light brown or dark blonde to light blonde hair with no reddish or orange undertones, you're likely a **light cool**. Light cools are usually fair-skinned without freckles, and they usually tan easily at the beach.

Pastels look great on light cools. Think lavender, soft pink, light blue, heather gray, and mint green.

A **warm skin tone** means your skin has orange-brown undertones. The veins on your wrist will appear greenish rather than blue. You'll likely have natural auburn or reddish highlights if you have brown hair, or you'll have deep auburn hair to medium red or copper hair. Dark warms can be a range of skin shades from very fair to olive to medium brown. To flatter this skin tone, go for camel, orange, gold, scarlet red, and mustard yellow.

Of course, these rules aren't hard and fast. If you're a warm skin tone and love your dusty pink sweater, by all means wear it! These are just some quick tips in case you've been playing it safe with colors (sticking with black, gray, and beige) because you're not sure which bold colors will look fabulous on you.

My one piece of advice? Step out of your comfort zone. Wear a color combination you normally wouldn't wear. Go and get a

color that pops; try royal blue leggings or red pants and match
them with a complementary color. Use the color wheel below to
pair colors (choose two on opposite sides of the wheel).

You'll see complementary colors paired in my Attitudes
by Renee tunics and maxi dresses: navy blue with a rust gold
pattern or yellow-green and red-violet flowers paired together.

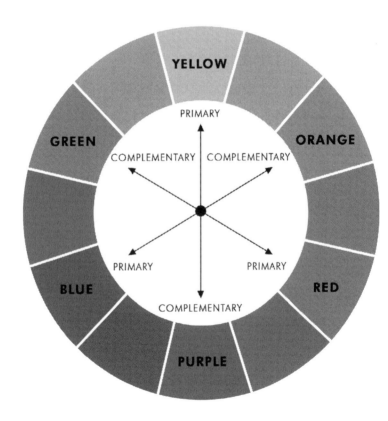

Even if your go-to color is black — and there's certainly nothing wrong with that — you can add a pop of color with a statement necklace, belt, or well-placed scarf to draw the eye to your décolleté or waist.

CLOTHING STYLES THAT FLATTER

My fashion collections are designed to look flattering on every body type. Once we have a sample of a new concept, I will literally try it on my team in the studio, who range in size from XS to 2X – regular and petite – to see how it looks and how it can be improved. Sometimes we need to adjust a sample two or three times before we place an order.

A lot of my ideas for new collections come straight from my travels to China, South Korea, Milan, London, and the Caribbean. As an avid traveler, I'm obsessed with the idea of being a Wardrobe Warrior helping women pack and travel with as much ease and as little bulk as possible. My Wardrobe Warrior collections go together, pack well without wrinkling, and fold up beautifully in your carry-on suitcase.

My travels inspire me. I'll see a beautiful fabric on a sheath dress worn by women in Seoul and will figure out how to adapt it into a refined como jersey dress for women in America. When I saw women in Paris wearing men's-style button-down shirts, I immediately thought of a way to tweak the trend to design a flattering big shirt that would work on all body types. I started a new collection of wrinkle-resistant shirts with attitude: a shirt with cuffs that tie into bows, and for the wow factor, I added a piece of elastic at the top back of the shirt to keep it in place, no sliding down in the front and no slipping backward.

I travel again and again to some countries, like South Korea, because the women there are really inventive and fashion forward. And I love that attitude! It epitomizes what I try to do with all of my collections.

The cuts of my collections are fairly standardized. My Women with Control pants are usually 86% cotton and 14% spandex for tummy control and to smooth out cellulite. All of my pants come in petite, regular, and tall sizes.

Most of the tops in my Attitudes by Renee collection are semi-fitted: more fitted in the chest, slightly looser in the waist, with a little flaring around the hips and a length that provides ample coverage in the back. I've found that A-line cuts flatter most body types, especially in fabrics that drape really well. I am also now known for my maxi dresses, full-length dresses that sweep down and flow lightly over the body, accentuating curves in the right places.

I stick with what women like, and let me tell you, I hear when things are and aren't working for them from my thousands of Wardrobe Warriors on social media. If they love something, they talk about it. If they *intensely dislike* something, they may talk about it even more! I cherish this social media feedback – and I respond to it. If something isn't flattering for our clientele, we stop making it.

One of my favorite Wardrobe Warriors, Monique Berry-Moore, gives me inspiration for new designs when I see how she puts together her outfits and posts them on the Wardrobe Warriors Facebook group page. She'll add a mock turtleneck in pastel pink or black one of my tunics to turn it into winter wear, and she will accessorize with gorgeous statement jewelry and an elegant shade of lipstick. She always strikes a model pose, resting her chin in her palm or leaning against the trunk of a tree. I look at her photos and think, "This is the Woman with Control who I'm designing clothes for."

Monique Berry-Moore, Wardrobe Warrior

As Monique describes my collections, "These clothes give us Wardrobe Warriors confidence and a sense of empowerment (for me for sure). I'm always getting compliments and asked all the time where I purchased my outfit."

Like all Women with Control, Monique has endured through life crises. At 24, while pregnant with her second son, she was diagnosed with a rare type of tongue cancer. She got through the treatments, has two healthy grown sons, and is still married to her high school sweetheart. "The most important thing is I'm alive, and God has allowed me to continue on with my life and to be here with my family."

I have to tell you, I feel grateful for women like Monique and all of the empowered Wardrobe Warriors who give me inspiration and feedback every day. If you are one of them, I thank you! If you're not a member yet, please join our community!

Here's how to find Wardrobe Warriors on Facebook:

facebook.com/groups/627976820933348/

And here's a link to my Instagram feed:

instagram.com/reneegreensteinqvc/?hl=en

DRESSING WITH A SENSE OF MINDFULNESS

I'm all about dressing to impress, but sometimes you're just not sure what feels right. You want to dress to feel a mood boost. You want to reflect your most authentic self. You want to feel a sense of power and command over any low points you're currently experiencing in life. What you're really looking for is dressing with a sense of purpose.

You're practicing mindfulness over your fashion choices.

Yes, I know. Mindfulness has become a huge buzzword for those who like to close their eyes and focus on breathing.

I'm not that type. I don't meditate, and I don't do yoga, though I know these can be incredibly helpful tools for millions of people.. But I do get dressed each day — sometimes multiple times a day — with mindful intent.

Mindful dressing is a movement that's gaining momentum, according to a recent article in the New York Post. The Fashion Institute of Technology has started offering fashion psychology classes about how color and clothing affect human behavior. University of Delaware apparel design and fashion merchandising majors now have a required course in the Social Psychological Aspects of Clothing.

It's no longer enough to just pop something on and say, "Hell, this looks damn good on me!" Now you need to figure out why you feel that way.

It's not a bad idea if you're into that sort of thing, because having a little self-awareness can help you strategically purchase clothes that will make you feel good when you put them on. It will also help you avoid expensive fashion mistakes.

Dawnn Karen, a brand consultant, therapist, and instructor at FIT, is a self-described "fashion psychologist" who teaches women to tune into the intersection of how they dress and how their clothing choices make them feel. She told The New York Times that her work is "styling from the inside out. Most of the time we go into our closet and say, 'I'll wear this color.' But we're not in tune with how we're feeling." She teaches her clients how to assess whether they're dressing in clothes that they use as an emotional crutch or a means of empowerment.

For example, Karen recently helped a widow who didn't realize she was still wearing only black, two years after her husband's death, learn to embrace color again as a way of coming to terms with her grief. Karen found that wearing elaborate, fashionable – even flamboyant – accessories, like huge feather earrings, gave her a sense of protection and healing after her fiancé assaulted her. And now she deliberately dresses down for her FIT students, sometimes wearing sweats to class in an effort to help her inner-city students understand that dressing down doesn't mean you're not smart or unsuccessful. She's deliberately making herself more relatable to help her students see themselves in her.

You can do a little of your own gentle probing: Why is that your favorite outfit? Why don't you like form-fitting clothes? If you find your clothes are stuck in a certain decade, probe for the reasons why. Was that the point in your life when you felt most at your peak? Do you feel younger or more alive when you wear a certain outfit from your teens or early 20s?

There may be things you can do to update your wardrobe while still retaining that sense of feeling strong and empowered. Also, keep in mind that while your perception may be your reality, others' perception of you is also a reality. They may see you as behind the times, which is probably not the impression you want to convey. It's all about striking the right balance or, as Karen says, "bridging the gap between internal and the external."

I love that concept, and I think it's the essence of what a Woman with Control does to make her style work for her.

CHAPTER 6

Roll with the Punches

People ask me all the time how I came up with "Women with Control" as the name of my QVC fashion collection.

Oddly, no one ever asks how I picked the name "Attitudes by Renee" for my collection of clothing and jewelry. Anyone who has seen my QVC show knows the name fits who I am. I am nothing if not positive attitude!

But Women with Control kind of makes you think, doesn't it? The name itself could be a mission statement or philosophy. But I think of it more like a challenge or overall approach to life. Whatever life throws my way, I'll respond in my own unique way — not out of fear, but out of strength. That's the kind of motto we should all live by, right?

Women with Control emerged from many facets of my life and personality. Sure, I was interested in designing clothing that provides control and can be worn as outerwear, not underwear. I did NOT want women to be confined to any corset-like shapewear that goes under a dress or pants and has literally caused women to feel nauseous or faint from discomfort and breathing difficulties.

Ick! Why do we need to return ourselves to the 19th century?

Talk show host and former supermodel Tyra Banks once wisely noted that women all have a "little something, something," no matter what size they are. It's true. We all have something we want to control.

As I hit my 30s, I began to notice a little wiggle and jiggle around my hips, butt, and belly. I recognized my imperfections, and I wanted clothes that would smooth out the lumps and bumps. But above all, I also wanted to be comfortable, and I wanted all women who wore my clothes to feel comfortable with a sense of freedom. I do not wear a shaper for this reason, and I didn't want other women to have to wear one either.

I did extensive testing with different fabrics and found tha 86% cotton and 14% spandex with four-way stretch and a matte finish — not shiny like activewear — was the perfect combination to keep you looking your best without sacrificing on comfort.

Let me say this again: No shaper needed!

Renee shopping for inspiration

'OMAN WITH CONTROL ≠ CONTROLLING WOMAN

I knew at the time what "Women with Control" meant to me. It was a state of mind that was embodied by a clothing line. These clothes were designed to help women feel a sense of mastery over their bodies. They were dressing themselves to look and feel their best — to give themselves a sense of power. While I understood this concept as a fashion designer, I also knew that the concepts could extend to a positive way of living and a calm state of being.

Being a Woman with Control means having control over yourself and how you respond to your circumstances. It does not, however, mean being a "controlling woman."

I do not control anyone but myself. Oh, I've tried, believe me. Ladies, haven't we all? I'd love to get my husband, my son, my grandkids, and my friends to behave and communicate with me exactly as I'd like, but I can't. I've been told I can't, and yeah, I've become a believer.

And it's made me a happier person. Trying to control other people and the world around you is as pointless as that guy pushing the rock up the hill over and over again, only to watch it roll back down every time.

It's sheer stupidity — and I just don't have the time to be stupid.

Okay, enough said about that.

WOMAN WITH CONTROL = EMPOWERED WOMAN

The concept of "Women with Control" has a deeper meaning for me. It's a positive message and one of empowerment. I believe it remains just as relevant as ever today in the #MeToo era, when women have opened up about abuse, sexual misconduct, and discrimination based on their gender.

But let's rewind a decade. Back in 2009, around the same time as I was getting ready to launch my fashion collection, I read the headlines and saw the shocking photo of *Billboard*-chart-topping singer Rihanna with a bruised and battered face. She was beaten by her then-boyfriend, pop star Chris Brown, who later pled guilty to the attack. I was shocked and disturbed by what I thought was an overly tolerant attitude by the media toward domestic abuse, given that 1 in 4 women will experience domestic violence at some point.

Rihanna spoke about the attack several months later, giving this advice on ABC's *Good Morning America*: "I will say that to any young girl who is going through domestic violence, don't react off of love. Eff love. Come out of the situation, and look at it in the third person and for what it really is."

If you're a victim of a violent relationship, there are resources out there that can help you get to a safe place. The internet is a good tool for locating shelters in your local area. The National Domestic Violence Hotline (1-800-799-SAFE) is another great resource.

Women with Control is my nod to women in need who are looking for empowering messages in their lives. No, a pair of great-fitting pants will not provide a way out of a violent situation, but each small step a woman takes to feel a little stronger and better about herself might help her summon the courage to change her life.

I also put my money where my mouth is by donating to organizations like Women in Need (WIN), which provides safe housing for women and children who are homeless, often after escaping from domestic violence. It's about helping women help themselves gain control over their situation and lives and to rise from the ashes of abuse.

WOMEN WITH CONTROL HAVE CHUTZPAH

Courage — or as my bubbie would say, "chutzpah" — is a key ingredient to success and, quite frankly, survival in life.

It's about rolling the dice and taking a risk. And it's embracing the fear and excitement that come with it.

In his best-selling book *David and Goliath,* Malcolm Gladwell talks about how challenges and disadvantages can work in our favor to make us more successful. He discusses the idea of "desirable difficulty," meaning that not all difficulties in life are negative. Sometimes, he writes, "that obstacle gives you the courage to take chances you would never otherwise have taken."

I can't help thinking that part of my own success stemmed from tragedy. I was left nearly penniless when my beloved first husband, Doug, died tragically from heart failure, a complication of his Hodgkin's disease. He had no life insurance and had run through our savings as he also had an illness of being a compulsive gambler. I had a young son to raise, an elderly father living with us, and very little savings in the bank.

I was a young woman, suddenly widowed, with an elderly father and a son to support.

Renee (left) and Doug (right) with their son Corey (middle) at his Bar Mitzvah

What the hell am I going to do? That was a question that ran through my mind a hundred times a day.

Although I had been earning a decent living working in sales in the New York fashion industry, we had been living beyond our means, and now I had no safety net. I felt like I was heading into a free fall, about to crash and burn.

I was dealing with the loss of my beloved husband, and my son was struggling to come to terms with life without his father. I couldn't just seal myself in my own grief. I needed to try to help my son through his.

We sold our luxurious condo and moved to a less-expensive rental in a nearby town as I tried to figure out what move to make next.

I went through all five stages of grief....and I lived by the serenity prayer:

"God grant me the serenity

to accept the things I cannot change;

courage to change the things I can;

and wisdom to know the difference."

I quickly learned that a person can survive anything, including going broke and being widowed. Fortunately, I had my career to fall back on. I had been working in sales and became a partner at a very successful fashion company. After Doug's death, I left to run a showroom working with department store buyers, and there I met my future business partner, Randie. My way of coming back was developing a new business. Randie and I started small: a new type of slinky fabric that we started selling to QVC. Somewhere deep down, I knew I had what it took to create and build a successful company. It might seem strange that I didn't doubt myself given all the roadblocks that life had thrown in my path, but I really didn't. I think that's the essence of being a Woman with Control.

GETTING A SHOT AT QVC

My dream started with Citiknits, a collection that I designed, developed, and manufactured for QVC. While QVC was buying the collection I designed, I left the company to start my own design firm, and QVC began buying from me directly. A few months later, a director at QVC saw a something in me that I never knew I had: a talent for selling directly to TV viewers on a live show. She encouraged me to go on air with Citiknits, and after my first appearance, it was obvious that I had a knack for connecting with my audience. The fashion collection became a very successful brand.

But I wanted more. I decided to develop my own fashion collection for the sophisticated city lady who traveled all over the world. The collection was seasonless, wrinkle-free, and packable. I called it "Attitudes by Renee," and I flew to London every few months to sell my collection on QVC UK.

A few years later, in 2009, I had my wiggles and jiggles *a-ha!* moment. I was getting older, my body was aging, and I needed a life-changing garment that that would smooth my lumps and bumps and erase any signs of cellulite — without the need for a shaper underneath. I came back to QVC in the United States and told them I had a great line of pants that I wanted to sell. I had created, designed, and trademarked an anti-aging, anti-gravity garment that would change women's lives and help them feel better about themselves. I knew these pants had the potential to improve women's lives because I had already been transformed by them myself.

The first day I went on air on the QVC USA channel, I was selling only two pant styles as part of my new Women with Control collection. One of the models at QVC stood there wearing my pants and started doing a little criss-cross dance, like my father used to do, crossing her arms over her knees and moving them back and forth. She repeatedly said, "Notice the benefit. Look, my sides don't shake, nothing shakes."

I looked into the camera and said, "Anyone who has a perfect body, call me now. But the truth is, none of us do. You can accept that you'll never have a perfect body and still feel great."

My goal was to show viewers how putting on a butt-lifting pair of pants that minimizes any jiggling will make women feel amazing, as well as stronger and more confident.

"No More Wiggle, No More Jiggle."

To make a long story short, the pants were a smashing success. We sold out quickly, and the rest is history.

Women wanted what I was selling. They were looking for clothes that would flatter their figure without sacrificing on comfort.

Renee and friends doing a live show on QVC

BELIEVING IN YOUR DESTINY

I'm a very spiritual person, and I think things happen for a reason. I truly believe that the tragedy of Doug's sudden death, the money challenges, and my leap into a QVC fashion collection were all written in the stars for me. I also believe it was destiny that brought me a new love, my husband Justin, soon after Doug died, but I'll talk more about that later. As we say in Yiddish, it was "*bashert*" (pre-destined).

I also think I needed to experience a life that was totally spinning out of control to recognize the importance of maintaining my own control over how I responded to tragedy, grief, and the threat of financial devastation. "Women with Control" became a mantra drumming through my head. I wanted to live my life with control, and I wanted other women to experience the blessing that comes with knowing that they can face any crisis and come out the other side as a stronger person.

Yes, I an

how I try

spinning in

en have of

tude of con

allowing a l

bringing yo ... ... of denial,

pretending everything is okay until you're ready to process and think through how you're going to cope.

You just need to OWN your situation and figure out what dance moves you'll need to get you through the song.

But know this: Being a Woman with Control doesn't mean you need to go it alone. I relied on massive amounts of love and support from friends, coworkers, and family when Doug died. They visited, called, brought me food, sent me cards, and helped clean out closets filled with Doug's clothes. They waited patiently for me to resume living again, to once again fill my house with fresh flowers.

Yes, I love fresh flowers, and I *always* ha

tulips throughout my house. Except

after Doug died. I couldn't bea

house. Flowers filled me

a while in my sadne

husband died.

tulips bac

was

ve vases of roses and

when I was in mourning

r to see a single flower in my

ith joy, and I just needed to sit for

s and grief. About eight months after my

friend of mine came over and saw the roses and

k in their vases. She said it was then that she knew I

going to be okay.

For years, I wore a pendant every day that I created for my Attitudes by Renee jewelry line. I called it "Life Is Half Full" because my father always told me to look at life as if the glass was half full, not half empty. This mantra has carried me through the highs and lows of my life. When I designed the pendant, I filled its glass rectangular shape halfway with beautiful gemstones of various colors, shapes, and sizes to represent all the friends and family who gave me the strength to remain positive through challenging times and have cheered my successes.

They were there for me when Doug died, holding me, hugging me, and just waiting patiently for me to work through my grief. And they supported me when Justin came into my life and brought the kind of joy that I never thought I'd ever experience again.

Renee with her Life is Half Full pendant

CHAPTER 7

Have Mastery Over the Frenzy of Life

How many times have you thought to yourself, "I'd really love to do _____, but I'm too busy!" I'm too busy to take a vacation. I'm too busy to visit my mom. I'm too busy to get to the gym, eat a healthy meal, go out for dinner and movie.

I get it. I do. I'm in the same boat, but I need fun and meaningful experiences in my life. So, I move whatever mountains I need to make time for them. Otherwise, what's the point of it all?

There was a time in my life (and there still are times) when I feel like I need to ask my Google calendar for an evening off. *Ridiculous, right?* What kind of weird voodoo power am I giving to this app? I feel powerless against it, even though I'm the one adding meetings and appointments — or giving scheduling instructions to my personal assistant.

Sometimes I literally need to remind myself that I am the one in control of my time. As a business owner, I actually have *more* control over my day than many people who have a boss to report to each morning. But let's face it. We can be our own worst bosses. We can drive ourselves as hard as we like, and who's gonna file a workplace complaint? As a result, I'm insanely busy — like All. The. Time.

And, yet, I still squeeze more stuff in. Like writing a book. That's because I truly believe time will expand to meet all of my needs. It will all get done. It has to.

How do I do it?

A lot of it lies in perception. I now make it a point to remind myself each day — okay, sometimes a few times a day — that I'm in the driver's seat. A Woman with Control has mastery over her schedule. Yes, it may be over-packed (which I would never do with my suitcase, BTW). Yes, it may mean that sometimes things need to slip. I frequently go without a manicure and rush to get one right before going on air. And, yes, sometimes I'll work through a meal or two and eat French fries and drink wine for dinner.

But I'm good with that.

I'm good with leading a busy life — no regrets. In fact, like many ambitious women, I thrive on a moderate amount of stress and the adrenaline rush of my work. I do not like to be bored.

And, yeah, I also have a hard time separating from my phone and can easily lose an hour absorbed in my Instagram and Facebook feeds. But I do NOT consider this a waste of time because it keeps me connected to fabulous women like you who have questions about my collections or who want to share their experiences becoming Women with Control.

Jeannee Robinson, 48, is one such amazing woman. She reached out to me on Facebook with a post that brightened my day:

"Thank you for helping me find my confidence again. Thanks to your designs and your attention to detail, I feel beautiful, professional and put together even though I'm not at my perfect weight. Thank you for helping me realize that I can be stylish, no matter what size I am. I've finally stopped beating myself up because of my body type."

Jeannee epitomizes my vision for Women with Control. I created the concept with women like her in mind. Her words affirm my mission and convince me that my fashion collections are helping women feel better about themselves and helping them get over the garbage fed to them by well-meaning friends or magazine editors. No, you really don't need a "summer work-out to get you beach-body ready." I always joke that there are two steps to getting a beach body:

1. Have a body.

2. Go to the beach.

Jeannee gets it. She doesn't let anyone take advantage of her; she can't afford to if she wants to be a Woman with Control and in command of her life. As a scheduler for defense and software contractors in Virginia, she's got her engines firing on all cylinders throughout her busy work day. "If a contract gets behind schedule, I get them back on. It's a pretty high-stress job, and I'm not everyone's favorite person," she said in an interview. "I work with geeky computer guys who wear hoodies and sneakers, but I also travel a lot for meetings on the business side with high-tech executives. I need to look the part — put-together and professional."

Kickass in every way, Jeannee used to be a competitive weight lifter. "I was all muscle, hitting the gym six days a week." But then her career became her top priority, and she dropped her workout regimen and found herself gaining weight. Before discovering my fashion collection, Jeannee lived in clothes from Lane Bryant and other plus-size fashion lines and just wasn't happy with her look. "I'm 5'3" on a tall day and heavy chested; I always felt like 'the girls' were coming into the room first, which I didn't want."

She happened to tune into QVC one April day in 2017 and saw me selling a new Women with Control fashion set with crop pants and a collared shirt. It was being modeled by women of all different shapes and sizes. "I thought, wow, that looks good on everybody," she said. "I ended up buying three sets in different colors. The pants are comfortable, I feel taller, my boobs no longer look enormous, and my butt looks great. I've now literally replaced 90 percent of my wardrobe with Renee's clothes. It makes mornings so much easier. I used to dread thinking about what I was going to put together to look appropriate. Now it takes me two minutes to pull together an outfit."

Jeannee has also made plans to get back into her old passion of weight lifting, despite her crazy work schedule. "I'm working on setting my own boundaries to allow myself time each day completely separate from work. I met with a coach, have a gym, and am working on a plan to lift two or three days each week."

Jeannee Robinson, Wardrobe Warrior

GETTING REAL WITH
YOUR BOUNDARIES

You can't be a Woman with Control if you don't have boundaries. People will walk all over you. Your boss, your friends, your parents. The special someone your life. Okay, I don't have as much of a problem with this. I'm pretty straightforward with the people in my life. They know I don't do sweet talk, and I don't feel guilty if I can't accommodate someone's expectations for me. If I really wanted someone to walk all over me, I'd try goat yoga. *Funny*

Um, yeah, not my thing.

Like any country or state, you need firmly drawn boundaries to establish who you are and how you want to take care of the territory of yourself. The United States of You.

What rules do you want for your country? What would you say in your own bill of rights? Who are the friendly nations? The enemies you'd like to steer clear of? What do you consider to be an invasion or unfair trade agreement?

I know this sounds silly, but boundaries are all about self-care, figuring out your priorities, what's worthy of your precious time, and what simply isn't.

"When we set boundaries in our lives, we feel more connected with ourselves and more in control of our lives. We are able to live for ourselves, rather than through this desire to please other people. We are able to be in relationships that are healthy, balanced, and equal," wrote relationship coach Jennifer Twardowski in a Huffington Post blog.

For me, boundaries are essential for determining how I want to spend my time. With so little free time, I choose to spend it doing things that are important and meaningful — as well as enjoyable. If it's not one of those three things, I don't do it. I will always find time to see my precious grandchildren, Princess Aya and Master Levi, on a Sunday for brunch. (Let the work emails wait.) I also go to my neighbor's cocktail parties with Justin because I have fun at them. I walk as much as I can (fun, relaxing, important for my health), but I don't go to the gym (not enjoyable for me, so I won't give up other stuff to do it).

Like so many women, you may feel like you never have enough time in the day. But I also think you can make time for whatever you want to experience or get done if you're cognizant of the boundaries you set for yourself.

So the next time you're asked to chair a PTA event or organize a bridal shower, think really hard about your boundaries: what's written in the constitution of the country called YOURSELF? Is this new commitment essential to you feeling joy or meaning in your life?

Unless it's really worth your time....

JUST SAY NO!

It may be hard for you at first because women have been taught to please others, but trust me, you'll be far happier as a result.

Here are the things that are worthy of my time:

1. My family

2. My work

3. My passions

I will fly to Florida to see my husband's family, whom I adore. I'll travel to Great Britain, France, Italy, Asia, the Caribbean — oh heck, pretty much anywhere in the world — for my business. I'll travel to see the colorful turbans and flowing fabrics of Jamaica and the prints in Tuscany to give me inspiration in my own designs. I'll take time to set a proper table with fine china, cloth napkins, and a vase full of flowers because I think visually appealing meals heighten the dining experience.

Renee and Justin

How to fit it all? Everything can be rolled up for an easier fit and no wrinkles. I roll my two crop pants together and tuck them into the corner of the suitcase, and I roll the leggings, tops, and jacket. I tuck my socks into my shoes, and I have a separate compartment for my jewelry and toiletries and voila! All packed.

My goal is to be casual and chic. Usually, I'

also taking some time for leisure activities, so

to do double and triple duty. It's all about having layers

satile pieces in neutral colors that can be mixed and matched.

Check out this link to my video for a quick packing tutorial.

youtube.com/watch?v=0sMQ60cTQgY

WIND-DOWN TIME

It may seem strange to have to schedule relaxation time. But wind-down time is an important priority for me every day. I need it, and I make time for it. Usually, it takes the form of a glass of wine as I'm sitting down to savor dinner. I place my napkin in my lap, pour a glass of red, and take a moment to gaze at its color, swirl it around to get a sense of its body and texture, smell it, sip it, and really experience the taste.

It's a mindful practice on par with meditation.

So why is wind-down time so important? It's like the period at the end of a sentence. You need a little self-care and reflection at the end of your busy day. Taking the time to relax before you sleep is an acknowledgement that you're nurturing and indulging in yourself. This is your "me time," and it's just important as your carpool, work, and relationship obligations. It's a reminder to yourself that you are a Woman with Control who understands the value of the candle-lit bubble baths or ginger tea moments.

How do you like to relax? Find your own method that soothes you and gives you pleasure, and do it every day.

Renee and her son Corey

CHAPTER 8

Find Love After Loss

When I was free-falling into a bottomless pit of grief after my husband Doug died, my close friends and family predicted I'd do one of two things:

    1. Climb into a cave and forget anyone ever existed

or

    2. Dance on the ceiling

I chose to dance on the ceiling. In other words, I needed to keep on living.

But it wasn't like that at first. In those early days of grief, I was happy to stay in my cave for a while.

During the traditional Jewish week of mourning, called

Shiva, I remember the rabbi from my synagogue coming to my house to make a shiva call. He sat with me and explained the laws of mourning.

For 30 days, I couldn't purchase or wear new clothes, couldn't go to any parties or weddings, and couldn't get a haircut.

That made sense to me. The truth is, I thought that 30 days wouldn't be long enough to mourn. I was in such a tailspin, and I didn't think the world would stop swirling around me in a state of utter chaos. I couldn't imagine things going back to "normal."

My friend Larry Scott visited me during shiva. He was 6′4″ and gorgeous, and he owned Larry and the Red Head, a restaurant in Great Neck, Long Island. He took one look at the crowd that had gathered around me, all my friends hugging me, holding my hand, offering their support and kind words, and he came up with a plan.

"How about we get this crowd to gather at my restaurant on Wednesday evenings?" he suggested to me a few weeks later. "We could have a Wednesdays with Renee night."

Larry had pinpointed what would become an important part of my healing process because he knew I was naturally social and craved human connection with friends and acquaintances.

He also knew I loved to meet new people.

At first I thought he was crazy because I couldn't imagine mixing and mingling, or even making small talk. I was haunted a thousand times a day by images of my beloved Doug having a heart attack and dying in front of me. How can *that* translate to light cocktail conversation?

But Larry persisted, and about three months after Doug died, I relented and did my first hostess night.

My friends all came, and so did a stranger who changed my life.

INSPIRATION IN A CARD

Before I get into how I met Justin, I want to tell you a little story about my yearly quest for the perfect New Year's card. I always send out beautiful greeting cards around the New Year to catch my friends and relatives up on my life and wish them good tidings in the year ahead. Doug and I used to go to the Jamie Ostrow stationery store on Madison Avenue to pick out something artful and inspiring with a meaningful message we wanted to convey. When I went to the store to get my cards after I became a widow, the salespeople hugged me and patted my hand as they kept showing me all kinds of sad and depressing cards — the kind that convey what a horrific and utterly devastating year I had.

I kept thinking, "Who the hell wants to get a card like this?" Finally I told the sales people to STOP! It was Doug who died, not me. They laughed a little nervously and then finally brought me the kind of cards I always sent: positive, inspirational, uplifting.

That was the kind of sentiment I wanted to convey. I knew Doug would have been proud I continued our tradition of trying to inspire and motivate the people I loved.

Perhaps that attitude explains my mindset when I stepped into Larry's restaurant to hostess that first night. This was my official first night "out" as a newly single woman. I was no longer attached — not by choice — but this was my new reality. I needed to move on.

Of course, I was also petrified. I got married in my late teens, and I thought I was permanently finished with the dating scene. Now, here I was in my 30s — a widow with a young son — putting herself out there. I had been nearly comatose for three months after Doug died, and now what? Would my friends

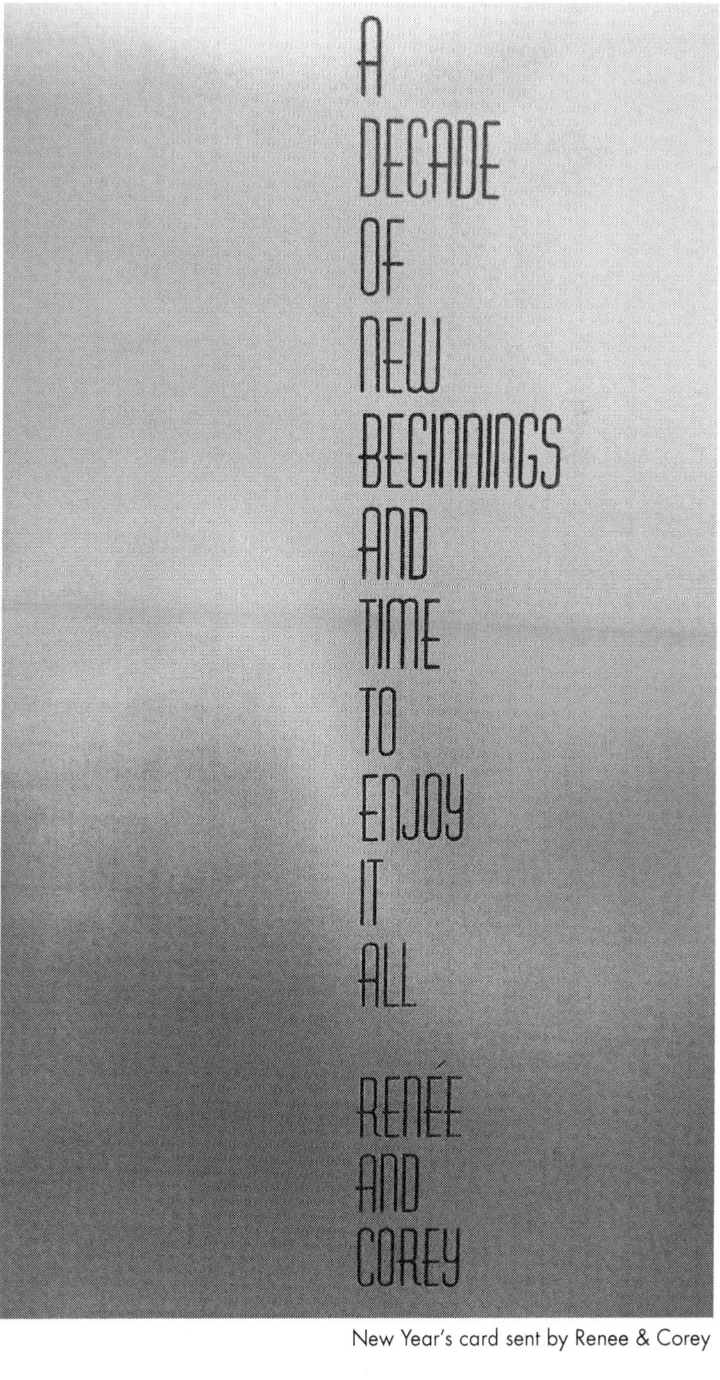

A

DECADE

OF

NEW

BEGINNINGS

AND

TIME

TO

ENJOY

IT

ALL

RENÉE

AND

COREY

New Year's card sent by Renee & Corey

accept me? Would their husbands act differently around me now, treat me as if I was now in the role of "saintly" widow?

I decided to dip my pinkie toe in the pool. It felt freezing at first, so foreign, but to my pleasant surprise, I was able to dive in pretty quickly. My heart was open, and I was ready to interact socially again. I wasn't ready to fall in love again quite yet, but I was open to making new friends.

From the moment I arrived at Larry's, I slipped right back into the old Renee. I greeted every patron with a smile and tidbit of conversation. I danced my way with them to their tables and sometimes sang along with the background music in the restaurant. The first night proved to be a pleasant distraction from my grief, and after a few weeks, I was beginning to feel a bit more alive again.

Then one Wednesday evening, a handsome gentleman with thick dark hair and dramatic brown eyes walked into the restaurant with a friend of his to get a beer.

I put my hand on his arm and said, "Hi, how are *you* tonight?" as if to say, "And who have we here?"

Justin looked at me as if I was from another planet. He wasn't use to someone being so warm and receptive to him. No, I wasn't coming on to him, but I guess he hadn't encountered too many friendly hostesses in New York. He told me later that he was immediately drawn in. Who was this exotic looking woman with the New York attitude? He was intrigued, this nice Jewish boy from Great Neck.

On our first date, I insisted on bringing a friend, so he did too. On our second date, Justin innocently took me to see a movie where the main character dies of a heart attack. After watching the scene, I started sobbing uncontrollably. *Great date, huh?*

Justin had no idea what was going on until I explained the circumstances of how Doug died. He expressed such in- credible compassion and understanding. I thought of him as a wonderful new companion and friend — in a *When Harry Met Sally* kind of way. At that point, marriage was the furthest thing from my mind.

Part of me still felt like dating was cheating on my husband. I was still crawling into bed every night pretending Doug was on a business trip when I saw the empty space next to me and the smooth, uncreased pillow.

Justin, not suffering from any recent romantic loss, was in a different place. By our third date, he knew he was going to marry me. This confirmed bachelor in his late 30s who had recently moved back to New York from Denver had done a complete 180 and was quickly ready to commit. I wasn't there yet, but I was suddenly having fun again, and I definitely wanted to keep seeing this new man in my life. Fortunately for me, Justin was patient, and he gave me the time I needed to open myself to new romance and love. He even wooed my father, who immediately loved him even though my father considered Doug to be like a son and was working through his own grief.

Renee and Justin on their wedding day

THE WISDOM OF WIDOWHOOD

Over the months, I acquired a kind of wisdom about widowhood. First, everyone mourns differently, and there is no set timetable for moving past your grief.

In living my life with control, I tried to find some kind of balance of grief and joy as the yin and yang of life. I needed to check in with my feelings daily and ask myself what it was I needed that day. I know I'm not a martyr, and I don't wallow. It's not who I want to be and certainly not the type of person I want to present to the world. My late husband was my best friend, and he gave me the confidence to get started in the fashion business. We were partners in every sense and were raising a son together. I knew a piece of me had been torn out and thrown away when Doug died and that I would likely always feel like I was missing that part of myself.

But I also wanted my life force back, and that meant feeling like a strong, desirable woman. Will I always have a part of me that mourns the loss of Doug? Absolutely. He still flashes through my mind at least once a day, even if I no longer feel the devastating ache that I once did.

Slowly over that first year of grief, I began to feel whole again — not like the same person I was when we were married, but like a new self. I had a deep wound, but there was a scab over it, and a scar was starting to form.

When you've been through the worst and you see you're still standing, you know you have real strength when the chips are down...

Coco Chanel believed in living life on her own terms, so why shouldn't the rest of us? "If you are sad, if you are heartbroken, make yourself up, dress up, add more lipstick, and attack," she advised.

That worked for her, and the way I dealt with my loss worked for me, but others may need other ways to process their sadness. Seeking professional help from a licensed grief counselor certainly can be helpful. I am not a doctor and do not want to dispense any medical advice. That said, you may want to see your doctor if your sadness lingers for weeks without lifting.

MOVING ON FROM A BREAKUP

While I went through the grief of widowhood, people going through a breakup or divorce can also experience profound anguish that's mixed with anger and bitterness. The death of a relationship is a loss. Period.

In one of my favorite scenes from *Waiting to Exhale*, one of my favorite movies, Angela Bassett finds out her husband is having an affair and is leaving her — after she abandoned her own dream of having a catering business so she could raise her children. She collects all of his clothes — suits, shoes, ties, shirts — stuffs them into his car, pours on some gasoline, and sets it all on fire.

Now that is a compelling revenge scene! But it's one that should remain in the pages of a novel or on the movie screen.

All women would be wise to stay within legal bounds if and when that one true love turns into that one true *hate*.

But a Woman with Control can still seek sweet revenge. I think an appropriate way to kick that cheater's butt is to slip on a little black dress and a pair of leopard-print heels, apply red lipstick, post a selfie of your gorgeous self on Facebook, and then hit a local nightclub. Make sure his friends know, because

— of course — by this point you've already cut him off from your social media.

But what if you find yourself staying home and — ugh — wallowing night after night? That is your grief taking control of you. And Women with Control do <u>not</u> let that happen.

Yes, you need patience and time to get over a loss, but a year? Two? For a relationship that lasted six months?

That's a problem.

BREAKUP THERAPY

I'm all about finding whatever it is that helps you feel alive again. You can spend three days at a "breakup bootcamp" if you'd like. Yes, these exist, according to a 2018 article in the "New York Times." The writer spent a weekend at a boot-camp retreat immersed in yoga, therapeutic workshops, and meditation sessions to help her become more conscious about her relationship cycles and more open to starting a new one.

This wouldn't be my first choice, but whatever works.

You can also try apps like Mend and RxBreakup and online relationship coaches like theheartbreakdoctor.com to help you move on and <u>not text your ex</u>.

Some Women with Control, like me, just sort of wing it and dive back into dating; others need professional help to move through and process their loss. There is no one best way to do this, but the right path should ultimately enable you to find love again after loss.

I was incredibly moved by the fascinating story of a young widow and widower who fell in love after connecting through the best-selling memoirs written by their dying spouses. John Duberstein promised his wife, Nina Riggs, author of The New York Times bestseller *Bright Hour*, that he would remarry after she died, and he found love again with Lucy Kalanithi, widow of Dr. Paul Kalanithi, author of the Pulitzer Prize-nominated memoir *When Breath Becomes Air*.

As Duberstein writes in a column posted on the website modernloss.com, "How do you manage the relationship to your new person while simultaneously learning how to have one with the original one? Because while loss may cut off your physical interactions, it couldn't possibly end your relationship, even if you'd somehow wanted that. There's that beautiful experience of being swept up in the emotion of new love, a phenomenon in itself. How do you keep that separate from lost love, so as to honor your ongoing relationship, while protecting your new love from feeling slighted or confounded with it?"

His advice for dealing with loving two people at the same time: We need to open ourselves up to the fact that we straddle the line between life and death while alive. If we can do that, we can manage two loves, the one in this world and the one in the next.

I think that's a beautiful way to frame things, and it's sort of the way I see the world. I also don't sugarcoat my loves. Doug had his issues. We had money problems and a risky way of living by the skin of our teeth, enjoying the fruits of our labor a little too much when we could have been more fiscally responsible.

Justin, on the other hand, was a bit too risk averse for me. He was very skeptical and worried about me starting my own business, and when I told him I was going to do it anyway, he said, "I'll give you six months. If you're not turning a profit by then, you have to promise me you'll go back to your former career."

Justin and I were newly married — still in that first rush of new love — so I couldn't believe he was also my biggest doubter! That can be REALLY TOUGH when it comes from the man you love who's supposed to support you.

Honestly, I didn't understand where he was coming from.

But maybe I benefitted from his doubt because, as I've said

before, I'm fueled by anger and my stubborn streak. I take all those no's and doors slammed in my face as challenges to take on and win — in my own way and in my own style. After all, that's what a Woman with Control does.

Renee and Justin

As you know, my business became a smashing success, and I have been happily saying, "I told you so" to my darling Justin ever since. He's actually the sweetest man I've ever met and has been my biggest cheerleader and supporter for years. He's an important partner in my business and the "chief operating rooster" — really the chief financial officer — of our corporation, Two Chicks in the Back Room.

Justin understands that there's a part of me — the part that still mourns Doug — that he will never have. But I think he has a better part of me.

So I'm happy I chose option #2, to dance on the ceiling. And I think Justin is too.

CHAPTER 9

Take Smart Risks

Women with Control take risks. We need to if we're going to get out there, take on the world, and pursue our dreams. There are, of course, potential pitfalls to any action we take, but as President John F. Kennedy once said, "They are far less than the long-range risks of comfortable inaction."

Comfortable inaction. It kind of makes you think of lying on the sofa, dozing in front of the TV, doesn't it?

Sure, you won't get run over by a bus while you're lying there, but you also won't have any positive impact on the world around you.

I could have chosen a life of comfortable inaction. I had a good job with a salary in the low six figures working as a partner at a small fashion company when I decided to a take leap and start my own business in 2001. I created CitiKnits, a fashion line made of slinky fabrics, that I sold to QVC. It was a risk to leave my comfortable, steady paycheck for a venture where I would be responsible for earning enough to make ends meet. Deep down I knew I could, but what if I didn't?

The truth is, I took a smart risk, not a stupid one. If I had started a dog-walking business or gone into day-trading, those would have been stupid risks. I don't have much experience with dogs or with financial investments.

But I did know a LOT about fashion. I had a knack for style, and people in the industry knew it. I had an eye for what works and what doesn't and a passion for wanting to dress women of all sizes to help them look their best.

I was fortunate to have a financial backer who knew me from the textile business and put up the funding for my materials and labor costs. He liked my spunk, liked how I negotiated prices on the textiles he sold me. He respected my ambition and drive — and loved how I dressed. He had faith that whatever clothing line I created would be a success.

But I was still taking a tremendous risk.

What if they went on air at QVC with my collection and it didn't sell?

I would be finished before I even got off the ground. If my conception about what women wanted didn't work, I would owe my backer thousands of dollars, but it was a career gamble I was willing to take.

CitiKnits was a hit, and I was able to exhale and enjoy the benefits of a risk that paid off well. But even now, I still feel my stomach churning a few minutes before I go on air to sell a new collection. I take risks every time I pitch a new collection. I know I can strike out with a dress or tunic that women just don't like. It's happened to me on several occasions, and I lost money. But I've hit many more home runs, and I couldn't have hit those without my strikeouts. And even now, with my great batting average, I get nervous about striking out.

When you hit that home run, wow, it's a great feeling. But it doesn't last long for me. And that's probably a good thing. My dad always said, "The minute you think you're smart, you're stupid." The moment your head starts to swell, you risk long-term failure because you start to ease back and coast a bit — and that's a sign of impending death when you're trying to grow a business.

THE SMART RISK EQUATION

Women with Control don't take stupid risks, so how can you tell the smart risk from the stupid one?

Tyler Tervooren, a writer who runs the popular website Riskology, came up with an equation to help you calculate whether the risks you take are smart and productive or dumb and destructive.

Here's how he describes it:

The two important variables are Potential Loss and Potential Reward.

Potential Loss means, "How bad will it be if there is a complete failure?" You might rate it on a scale from 0 to 9 with 0 being no loss at all and 9 being some sort of horrible, unacceptable loss.

Potential Reward means, "What's the outcome if there's success?" You can rate it on the same 10 point scale with 0 being no reward and 9 being a life-changing, nearly unfathomable reward.

Risk Quotient = Potential Reward ÷ Potential Loss

Tervooren defines a smart risk as any one where the risk

quotient is greater than 3. Anything below that is a stupid risk because the potential for loss is much greater than the potential for reward.

Think of it like this. Let's say you want to try a new hair stylist who charges $50 less for a haircut than your favorite stylist, who always gives you a great cut. The potential reward may be $50 saved but the potential loss could be a bad haircut that takes months to grow out. Is the potential reward worth it?

It may be; it depends on how much you rate the loss compared to the reward. You might need that $50 to pay your electric bill, for example, which would mean the reward has a much higher rating than the loss. Or you might not miss the $50 very much, which would give it a lower rating.

You can use this equation and apply it to any aspect of your life. Should you invest in cryptocurrency? Marry your boyfriend? Take a job in a new town?

THINK ABOUT RISKS GOING RIGHT RATHER THAN WRONG

When I launched my own business, I knew in my mind and in my heart that having my own fashion collection was a passion of mine that I would fulfill. Sure, I was nervous about taking the risk but I also pictured everything going ~~wrong~~ RIGHT.

That's something Tyler Tervooren did when he opted out of his career in the construction industry and started writing full time for his website. Thinking about things going right, instead of going wrong, is likely to get you more excited about your ideas "in a way that will breed success rather than failure," he says. Focusing on finding a life purpose in a new career, thinking about making a ton of money — like enough to buy a Jaguar — or fantasizing about meeting new people who will rock your world can all be huge motivators that push you to reach your goals.

For Deby Wine, a decision to take a life-changing risk centered on her desire to live a healthier life. After tipping the scales at more than 300 pounds, the grandmother of two from Virginia found that her obesity — which she'd been battling since she was a kid — had completely taken over her life. She decided to have gastric bypass surgery to shrink her stomach and help her lose weight.

"I had arthritis, Type 2 diabetes, high blood pressure, and an irregular heartbeat from sleep apnea," she says. "For a long time, I didn't go to the doctor because I didn't want to hear that I needed to lose weight."

But then came the painful foot fractures, 25 in all, including one where she broke her ankle simply standing in line at the grocery store. Deby decided that the potential reward of better health was far greater than any potential loss, like having to adjust to new eating and exercise habits and the risk of the surgery itself.

Now, four years later, Deby has lost more than 100 pounds, is down to a size 12, and has embraced a new sense of self. She's a certified support group specialist for people who have gone through gastric bypass surgery and is active all the time with gardening, mall walks, and home improvement projects like installing hardwood floors and gutting her bathroom. Where Deby used to only wear khakis and plain white t-shirts, she now has a full array of outfits from the Attitudes by Renee and Woman with Control collections.

"After losing 100 pounds, I had a lot of extra skin and sagging, but that all disappears when I slip on Renee's clothes. No more skin in between my thighs, sagging butt, or stomach. It all gets sucked in and pulled up. I feel great. I get an emotional boost and think 'I can do this.' I no longer feel helpless and hopeless."

Deby Wine, Wardrobe Warrior

WITH SUCCESS COMES "IMPOSTER SYNDROME"

Okay, let's say you take that risk and are a smashing success. Fantastic, right? Not always. Many of us have a hard time feeling successful. Instead, we feel like fakes, like we somehow didn't earn their accolades. Yes, even Facebook Chief Operating Officer Sheryl Sandberg admitted in a television interview, "There are still days I wake up feeling like a fraud, not sure I should be where I am." A year after that interview, she wrote in her best-selling book *Lean In*, "We hold ourselves back in ways both big and small, by lacking self-confidence, by not raising our hands, and by pulling back when we should be leaning in."

Too often, we attribute our accomplishments to luck or kind mentors who took us under their wing. Maybe it's the way girls are raised — to be modest, sweet, and humble.

Or maybe we just don't think we deserve the good things we get.

I always felt a little inferior because I don't have a college degree. Would I really be able to run my own business without a diploma with my name on it? But then I think of Steve

Jobs, Oprah, Ted Turner, and Ellen DeGeneres. All of them, like me, dropped out of college, but you'd never know it from their successes.

Sure, college is a worthwhile endeavor — often essential these days to get started on a career. But we shouldn't knock those who are self-taught and who expand their intellectual horizons by observing and learning from the world they experience. Most of my business acumen is something I would never have learned in an MBA program. But, honey, my toughness and street smarts have served me well!

I just had to get out there, take the plunge and work my butt off. In fact, I haven't slowed down. Not even a little bit.

Jeannee Robinson, who I mentioned in Chapter 6, told me she took a leap of faith and relocated from the Philadelphia suburbs to Connecticut for a career switch from working for a defense contractor to working in the biotech industry. She was recently divorced, mourning the death of her two parents, and looking for a new life. Well, it was a disaster. "It felt like a train derailment. I had no support system," she said, since she had few friends in her new town. She developed anxiety and depression from her "unhealthy" work environment and wound up seeking counseling from a therapist. The next risk she took was a smarter one: A new job in a more familiar field that was challenging and enabled her to excel as a contract scheduler.

"I found my way back to myself and after two years, my self-confidence is back." The moral of Jeannee's story is that you can take a risk and make a huge mistake and still bounce back. Her mistake led to an even better opportunity and a happier life.

FAILURE IS PART OF TAKING RISKS

Most of us can relate to Jeannee's experience and respect her for taking those chances. I know I do. We all take risks. If they don't work out, tough luck. You pick yourself up, brush yourself off, and get at it again. Failure is part of the deal.

But it's not the end of the game.

The best of us screw up. (I did, lots of times, and I still do from time to time.) The key is to understand and learn from our failures. That's part of being a Woman with Control.

In fact, sometimes failure can actually help us — by forcing us to adapt and improve.

The most successful innovators of our time, including Apple

founder Steve Jobs and Amazon founder Jeff Bezos, considered their failures to be important experiences on the path to breakthroughs. Thomas Edison didn't consider his first attempts at inventing the lightbulb to be failures. "I have not failed 10,000 times," he famously said. "I've successfully found 10,000 ways that will not work."

Bottom line: You take a risk. You fail. Then you triumph.

But what if you don't want to fail? What if you're terrified at the prospect of failure? I get it. Believe me.

Fear of failure is a real thing, and it can completely sabotage any chance you have of making those killer dreams come to life. Psychologists say it's not really about avoiding failure or the disappointment, anger, and frustration that come with it. It's about avoiding a deep sense of shame that ultimately makes you feel bad about who you are.

And, yeah, it can go hand in hand with that other little monster I mentioned: imposter syndrome.

No one wants to be exposed as a fake. "Pay no attention to the man behind the curtain! The Great Oz has spoken!" Yeah, right!

In a blog post for Psychology Today, Dr. Guy Winch writes that there are two steps to dealing with a fear of failure:

1. Own the fear.

2. Focus on aspects that are within your control.

Realizing that you have this fear, talking about it with others, and having self-awareness about feelings of shame you may have if you do fail can actually help you deal with these feelings. Taking charge of the stuff that you have some control over — like developing a budget, setting goals, and preparing for setbacks — can help you feel like you've got your act together.

I think there's a third way to slap some sense into yourself to get over your fear of failure. It's something they do in the tech world: failing fast.

Failing fast for a computer geek means it's better to roll out a probably adequate product quickly and then improve it than to tinker for months or years until you create perfection — and then realize your product is out of date or a competitor beat you to it. Make it "good enough," get it out, respond to feedback, and make small improvements along the way.

If you've got a bunch of tiny failures that ultimately lead to a superior product, you'll get yourself into the game quickly, and you'll remain a star player.

Of course, you shouldn't be selling schlock. Whether you've invented pantyhose that don't run, a suitcase you don't need to unpack, or a flexible sports bra — all recognized by Time magazine as the best inventions of 2018 — your first efforts still need to be *good enough*.

World-famous cellist Yo-Yo Ma says it all comes down to passion. "Passion is one great force that unleashes creativity, because if you're passionate about something, then you're more willing to take risks."

I truly believe that in my heart. No question, I've had my share of failures. I've designed dresses that I thought would be incredible and flattering for all body sizes, and my customers took one look at what I was selling — and passed. But I've had many more smashing successes from the risks I've taken. Expanding my line into denim was one of them. Yes, I keep on making those small iterative improvements — reversible fabrics or a two-piece collar that stands up. And, yes, I still get nervous every time I take a real risk, but that excitement also fuels me and makes me feel alive.

The truth is, I enjoy taking those chances every single day. My smart risks — whether they turn out to be successes or failures — are the reason for my success.

CHAPTER 10

Reinvent Themselves

In the movie "Second Act," Jennifer Lopez plays the role of a 40-year-old superstore manager who gets so angry after being passed over for a promotion that she quits and jumps into a new career — as an executive consultant for a high-end cosmetics company.

How kick-ass is *that*? Okay, I'm not saying you should use her tactics: She falsifies her resume by listing degrees from Harvard and Wharton, even though she never went to college.

But I do think that a Woman with Control reinvents herself. Again and again and again.

Reinvention keeps life interesting, and who the hell wants to be bored?

Reinvention keeps YOU interesting, and who the hell wants to be boring?

"You're never too old to set another goal or dream a new dream," best-selling author C. S. Lewis said. He was in his 50s when he dreamed up the Narnia fantasy world in his cherished novel *The Lion, the Witch and the Wardrobe*.

I can totally relate, since I still haven't stopped dreaming. Not by a long shot.

Reinvention comes in many forms, and your definition of it may be very different from mine. There are, though, some universal practices for getting it right. To successfully reinvent yourself, you'll need to take smart risks, as I discussed in Chapter 9.

And you'll need to fully embrace the possibility of change.

Every time some major setback happens in your life, you have the opportunity to reinvent yourself. Fired from a job? Get a better one. Jilted by a lover? Find someone better. Forced to move to a new city? Get a better apartment.

Are you starting to get my point here? Turn the sour lemons life throws your way into a thirst-quenching lemonade. You were meant to begin again. *Own* your decision to change, rather than feeling like change was forced on you.

That is the key to how a Woman with Control reinvents herself.

I've reinvented myself many times over the course of my life. I went from college student to fit model in the fur industry at 17. I got married and became a mother before I turned 20. I was a widow in my 30s, and I went through several career shifts in the fashion industry before launching my QVC collections. I'm still exploring new facets of my identity. I'm a book author. I'm relishing my time as a grandmother.

Renee and granddaughter Aya

I have so many plans bubbling up in my head that I'm never sure which ones to execute first.

Pushing myself to continually evolve brings me joy.

My motto: If you believe in what you want to do, go do it. And always keep your ultimate aim in mind.

For example, I haven't changed my mission in the past 10 years, even as I conjure up new designs for my collections. My purpose in fashion is to make women feel happier about themselves by providing them with clothes that flatter — without any need for an uncomfortable shaper. I also want to give women a way to travel to their heart's content by providing them with light, packable, fashionable items that won't wrinkle, can be worn in any season, and are very versatile.

I keep my eye squarely on my goals as I take on new projects like home renovations or writing to express my ideas to women as special as you.

ARE YOU READY FOR REINVENTION?

While the need for reinvention may come from an unexpected life circumstance, you've got to be ready to make a real change before you completely upend your life.

Sometimes, it's just not the right time. I must confess that I wouldn't have been able to break out and start my own business right after Doug died. I could barely get out of bed and get through my work day. I certainly wasn't in a creative frame of mind to think about launching a new clothing collection.

Becoming a widow changed me and gave me a new perspective on life, but it was thrust on me unexpectedly, and I needed to work through my grief on my own timeline. I didn't choose it and how I changed wasn't intentional.

Once I reinvented myself, however, I was truly ready and made a conscious decision to take a risk and try something new.

With reinvention, you are making a choice to undergo a metamorphosis, hopefully from a caterpillar into a butterfly, and not the other way around.

Renee and Jamie

Ask yourself three questions:

1. Am I feeling resilient? Some of us have a greater ability to bounce back from setbacks than others. But I also think there are times in our lives when we're feeling less resilient and — to be blunt — buried six feet deep under a ton of garbage. If you feel like you've got a good handle on life challenges and understand that most hardships you encounter will be temporary and surmountable, you've probably got a hefty dose of resilience that will help you successfully reinvent yourself.

2. Do I have enough support? You will need a team of friends and loved ones surrounding you to help you get through the tough early days of change. Change means challenge, and you need people you can really lean on. I had my spouse Justin, my business partner Randie, and a ton of friends that I could count on when I started my business. They tolerated my venting — hell, my rages! Being creative and innovative isn't easy; being a perfectionist, like I am, can be a downright curse. I would not have succeeded without my support system, and I truly think every woman needs a great team supporting her.

3. How is my self-image? You need to really believe in yourself and what you can do. I was able to picture myself as the queen of a line of control fashion wear before I ever stepped foot in the QVC studio. I knew my collection would be a slam dunk because I loved the design and knew it made me look my best; I knew my pants would truly make any woman feel beautiful and sexy.

Reinvention can also be something as simple as creating a new look. As a makeup artist for Estee Lauder, Ellen Murphy spends her days helping women transform themselves — creating contoured lines and smooth complexions with a few strokes of her brush. But the 41-year-old mother had been feeling uncomfortable and insecure in her own body for years. She knew she needed a new fashion style to help her feel more professional and polished in a field that focuses on enhancing a woman's natural beauty.

"I had several abdominal surgeries for medical reasons and wound up with an awkward-shaped stomach," Ellen explains. "I also have hips and a booty, so finding jeans that fit me well was really hard. I wanted to look trendy but also wear something age appropriate, both of which are crucial for my job."

After her mother-in-law introduced her to Women with Control on QVC, Ellen transformed her style.

"Like with makeup, you need a perfect foundation to your wardrobe, and I found that with the Women with Control leggings and pants that I wear on a daily basis," Ellen says. She pairs them with an Attitudes by Renee blouse or a faux-leather-sleeve blazer and — *poof!* — she feels like a new person. "I feel really great when I wear these clothes. Women in society do feel down when we don't look a certain way. Those clothes give empowerment back to women."

Hearing Ellen's story gives me goosebumps. I LOVE that she has been able to shed the negative feeling she had about her body by choosing to wear clothes that flatter and enhance her best parts. I love that she feels like a new person after making some tweaks to her wardrobe.

STYLE ISN'T ABOUT SIZE. IT'S ABOUT ATTITUDE.

I understood from my work as a fit model that our bodies change over time and we need to have clothes that adjust.

Wearing clothes that make you look your best can actually be transformative, as I'll explain in more detail in the next chapter. Having a style that works for you can enable you to feel confident enough to reveal new aspects of yourself, which is the first important step towards reinvention.

Psychologists point out that most of us, women especially, modify our identities as we go through our adult lives. "Even at 60, people can resolve to make themselves more the people they would like to become," said UC Berkeley psychologist Ravenna Helson in an interview with Psychology Today. Her evidence comes from a study that's been tracking female graduates of Mills College for the past 50 years to learn about how they've developed and shaped their lives through the decades. The latest results involving 100 participants who are still alive suggest that about 10 to 15 percent of women show substantial positive personality changes from ages 60 to 70.

Zoe B., a lifestyle coach who runs the website Simple Life Strategies, pointed out that many of the most successful people on the planet didn't hit their stride until much later in life:

At age 23, Oprah was fired from her first reporting job.

At age 24, Stephen King was working as a Janitor and living in a trailer.

At age 28, J.K. Rowling was a suicidal single parent living on welfare.

At age 30, Harrison Ford was a carpenter.

Vera Wang failed to make the Olympic figure skating team, didn't get the Editor-in Chief position at Vogue, and designed her first dress at 40.

Alan Rickman gave up his graphic design career to pursue acting at age 42.

Samuel L Jackson didn't get his first movie role until he was 46.

Morgan Freeman landed his first MAJOR movie role at 52.

Louise Hay didn't launch her publishing company, Hay House until she was 62.

"If you haven't found your dream career yet, it's not too late," she wrote in a Facebook post. "You aren't a failure because you haven't found fame and fortune by the age of 30. Hell, it's OK if you don't even know what your dream career is yet."

I can't stress enough how wonderful it can be to reinvent yourself. But I also can't stress enough how hard it can be to do it successfully, especially if you're planning a major life makeover. If only we could simply ask Tinker Bell to sprinkle a little pixie dust to make us fly. Every woman I know would love a Tinker Bell in her life! But that's just a fairy tale, and we need to be realistic. It takes planning and hard work to move forward and evolve into the latest version of yourself.

Here's some advice that I've found really helpful as I contemplate — even now — new ways to reinvent myself.

- **Take a deep dive into you.** Be honest with yourself. What are you really good at? What are your weaknesses? If you're a terrible writer, do not quit your accounting job to write the great American novel. You'll fail. (Sorry, I know the truth sometimes hurts.)

- **Work to reach your own unique potential.** "There's a lot of confusion and dissatisfaction out there at every stage of a person's career. Being happy in your career has more to do with reaching your unique potential than it does with meeting the definition of success that's set by everyone else," says Robert Steven Kaplan, Harvard Business School Dean, in *What You're Really Meant to Do*. It's about knowing your own story, looking at what's going on in the world around you, and matching yourself up with opportunities.

• **Personalize your definition of success.** Part of reaching your potential, Kaplan says, means creating your own definition of success. It's hard because society defines success for us: $1 million in your bank account; Mercedes in your driveway; 100K Instagram followers. You need to push away society's definitions of success and figure out how to reach your own potential. Determine your own measures of success and how to build on your unique talents and gifts. If you truly follow that path, you'll find you never fully reach those goals. You'll just keep growing and reinventing yourself. For example, if you make a plan to get in shape and transform your body, you will quickly realize that fitness isn't an end goal that you achieve and then stop. It's a constant process that requires you to keep working your butt off.

• **Figure out what matters most to you.** Reinvention is a process of self-discovery. You can't look at me and say, "Oh Renee's rocking it with her Women with Control collection, let me do that too." Bam! Game over. And don't listen to that friend who's pressuring you to help her fulfill her own dreams. You've got to figure out what YOU want and then go with that. Ultimately, you're letting go of old dreams to find more meaningful ones.

• **Get ready to work really, really hard.** "Reinventing yourself in your career is difficult. It doesn't happen on schedule, and it doesn't happen without a great deal of effort," says Art Petty, who runs the Management Excellence blog. He offers two more tips: Don't make your hobby into a business; most of the time it's a disaster in terms of making it marketable. At the same time, you can actually manufacture passion within yourself to create "something that is both marketable and in sync with your best abilities," he says. Hitting that sweet spot may take some experimentation — and guidance from a mentor.

• **Talk to the experts.** Being a Woman with Control means you plan ahead and try to learn as much as possible before launching a new career or life project. Talk to people who have already reached the goal you've set. If you're thinking about getting your real estate license, talk to successful brokers. If you're starting an online party business, reach out to people who already have one to determine what they wish they'd done differently when starting out. If you want

to become a foster parent, speak to — okay, you're getting it now.

Any successful woman can share her reality with you — both good

and bad — and this knowledge will serve you well.

CHAPTER 11

Enjoy Life to the Fullest

I'm asked fairly frequently about how I've been able to maintain my size-4 figure and smooth, glowing skin through the years. Do I work out every day? Do I live on a diet of kale smoothies, tofu, and steamed vegetables? Do I get 8 hours of sleep every night and meditate to avoid stress eating?

Honey, I wish I could say, yes, yes, yes! I live like a Buddhist monk. But honey, I'm not a liar.

The truth is, I could have much healthier habits.

Do you want to know my secret for maintaining my clothing size through the years?

So do I!

No, seriously. I have a few ideas. Some of it may be good

genes, but I also think my busy lifestyle keeps me literally on the run throughout the day. Sometimes I forget to eat three meals a day. Remember, I once struggled with anorexia. So I still weigh myself at least once a week and am careful to keep my weight fairly steady. Having had this illness, the fear of gaining weight remains in my mind.

When I'm stressed — which is every day — I don't necessarily go to my comfort foods, which are salty chips, popcorn, and fries. In fact, I tend to lose my appetite. But that's just me, and I realize that every one of us has a different food relationship story to tell.

Many of us eat to relieve stress or boredom or fatigue. Some of us use food as a drug to make us feel good. And all of us can overindulge when we're really passionate about what we're eating. The sheer joy triggered by the sweet, savory, spicy, or salty is something we don't want to end — so we eat to our heart's content.

And that's perfectly fine. Just don't do it every day.

A Woman with Control has a full awareness of her relationship with food and the finer luxuries of life. She owns her strengths and weaknesses and finds strategies for allowing herself to really savor her indulgences.

I know that I regularly skip meals, but I make a point to sit myself down for a proper meal at least once or twice a day — with a napkin on my lap and a full place setting with real dishes and silverware. And when I travel, I take the time to savor meals at my favorite restaurants, like Paper Moon in Milan, Sexy Fish in London, or La Petite Maison in Nice.

But I'm also trying to work more healthy activities into my routine in ways that allow me to feel like I'm savoring the rare precious time I have to myself. I take time to decompress. I might relax on the sofa catching up on the latest issue of Architectural Digest while sipping a glass of sauvignon blanc.

I also use plane travel as relaxation time. Yes, I know it sounds strange because most people despise air travel these days with the cramped seating and security hassles. But I treat it as "me time." I find it so relaxing that no one can get hold of me when I'm 30,000 feet in the air. I'll look out the window, binge on movies, sip Champagne, and catch up on my emails.

The joke is that everyone knows when I land because an explosion of emails from me hits their inboxes simultaneously once I get service back and my emails are sent.

I've gotten better about fitting more fresh fruit and vegetables into my life. (That's me, taking a little bow as you applaud.) At least one of my meals each day includes a green chopped salad or steamed broccoli or vegetables like spinach sautéed in garlic. I love a good chopped salad when the produce is crisp, colorful, fresh, and not soggy from dressing or mayonnaise. I usually get my dressing on the side, and just drizzle a bit on. I also add a thick, juicy protein I love like grilled steak, salmon, shrimp, or chicken.

Okay, let's get real now. My careful eating habits go only so far. I totally enjoy indulging in certain foods that soothe me or give me near orgasmic bursts of pleasure.

Sorry, but there's no other way to describe my love affair with French fries. Give me that perfectly crisp delicacy, fresh from the fryer, with a trace of oil, sprinkling of salt, and just the right puff of potato in the middle of that crispness. My mouth is watering right now just thinking about them.

I could eat a large plate of fries anytime, anywhere. But I treat them like an indulgence. I don't eat them every day.

In fact, I do this with the other pleasures in my life, too. I'm happy to partake, but I know I can't every day. When I indulge in fries, they'd better be perfect, or damn near it. I want to fully savor the experience, and you can bet I'm going to get the large size and really enjoy them. That's why I don't have my fries all that often. I want the novelty of the rare experience and am picky about my pleasures.

I think my attitude on this extends to other luxuries. Yes, I may be the first person to call French fries a luxury item — a medium at Burger King costs about $2. But I define luxury and indulgence based on the amount of pleasure you derive from it. Fries, to me, are decadent, and I have a ritual with Justin that we stop at Burger King and get an order of fries to share on our drive from New York City to West Chester, Pennsylvania, where QVC is located.

How much joy do YOU get out of the touch, taste, feel, or sight of something you love? I have no trouble comparing the experience of eating that perfect fry with the joy I felt, as a 15-year-old, when my aunt bought me my first Epi bag from the Louis Vuitton store in Paris. I loved the feel of the leather and considered it the most beautiful item I'd ever owned. It made me fall in love with luxury and appreciate fine quality.

But in the end, pleasure is pleasure is pleasure. Being a Woman with Control means you indulge in what gives you pleasure — in a smart, savvy way that won't hurt your emotional, physical, or financial health.

Buying a $1500 Louis Vuitton handbag or leasing a Mercedes SUV can bring you total, utter joy. And, honey, if you've got the financial means, by all means indulge. But you might need to settle for a less expensive luxury, maybe a $150 Coach bag or Toyota Rav 4, to indulge within your budget. The same goes for food pleasures. I know I won't damage my waistline if I savor those fries once a week, but I'd likely gain weight if I ate them every day. If you must have that piece of rich Godiva chocolate every day, have it, but stick with one piece. If you know that you'll eat the whole box, have that special chocolate only on rare occasions.

Sure, this is common sense, but there's also some new science that backs me up. I've talked a bit about mindfulness and self-awareness in previous chapters — how important it is to think about how you dress, the colors you choose, and the image you present to the world.

Gentle reminder: It does matter how you dress and what impression you make on the people in your life.

Well, those same concepts can be applied to savoring your food or shopping for life's luxuries. If you slow down and gratify yourself in a more deliberate way, you will not only enjoy the experience more, but you will likely be far more satisfied with less.

To me, this is an essential part of being a Woman with Control. If you are fully present and aware — savoring every moment that you indulge — you'll improve your health, and bonus, even your bank account.

MINDFUL EATING

A bunch of studies support the idea of living mindfully, and I think the evidence is strongest for mindfulness to prevent weight gain or to lose a few extra pounds. If you're eating mindfully, you're noticing the colors, smells, flavors, and textures of your food. You chew slowly, aren't reading texts or watching TV, and are not even having a conversation—except to comment on the tastes you're experiencing.

I don't eat to eat or to survive. I eat to enjoy. I will send a steak back if it's not medium rare and delicious. I'll send it back if it's tough or dry. I need to savor the texture and taste of my meal, or I simply won't eat it.

I love cooking. Julia Child was one of my inspirations. I use ingredients that are fresh, with colors that pop, and I grow my own garnish. Edible flowers are abundant on the deck of my country home in Pennsylvania, and I have containers of herbs under my kitchen window in Manhattan. I consider any food I serve to be part of my artistic vision, a palette of colorful delights.

My guests should expect to see perfectly plated salmon, in all its pinkness, accented by a sprinkling of green parsley, and accompanied by couscous mixed with bright yellow corn and perhaps some dried cranberries or pine nuts. No table would be complete without fresh cuttings of begonias from my garden in a crystal vase as a centerpiece. Like a set designer for the theater, I'm all about setting the stage for the dining experience. A fine artistic arrangement enhances the taste of the food.

And, yes, I want my guests to *kvell* over my table arrangements and plating of the food. Nothing gives me greater pleasure!

If you come to my home, it should be an experience. You will be served on the finest plates and silverware with fine stemware so you can fully enjoy the food, rather than eating just to satisfy your appetite. But I will not cook you a well-done steak. Please don't ask me to; I just can't. Instead, I'll offer you chicken or pasta because I need to give you perfection, and a juicy steak cannot be cooked to a brown crisp.

MINDFUL EATING:
HOW I EAT MY STEAK

Appreciating a perfect piece of steak is an art form. I'll look at it. It needs to look juicy, and it should be sizzling. I'll smell it. It has to have that smoky, roasted-meat aroma. When I cut into it, it needs to give easily, and I want to see that medium-rare red color. (I like my meat as I like my men — alive!) I will place a forkful on my tongue and chew slowly, really savoring the taste and chewy texture. If I'm not fully satisfied with that first bite,

I will put my fork down and won't eat any more. It's just not worth it to me to eat a less-than-satisfying meal.

MINDFUL SHOPPING

I've already mentioned that my first husband had a love for the finer things in life and often purchased things we couldn't afford, like fancy cars, jewelry, and clothes. When he died, I needed to come up with a new money blueprint to help me handle my finances correctly. Don't get me wrong — I didn't cut out all luxuries in life! But I did wait until I had enough money before I bought them. This is something Justin taught me. We don't carry credit card debt. We pay off our bills on time. I remember how triumphant I felt when I bought my first Jaguar after I became a partner in a fashion company. That was my dream car — my ultimate symbol of success. I knew when I had saved enough money to purchase it that I had arrived. I savored it. Just like I savor a perfect steak. (Okay, maybe a teensy bit more. It was a Jag after all, but you get what I mean.)

For me, a fine fabric is about the softness of the cloth against my skin. Whether it is a buttery leather, fine cotton, or smooth silk, it should invigorate the senses.

One of my mottos is that life is not a dress rehearsal. You need to live for today. You should be buying and enjoying the indulgences you can afford.

That's why I sell my collections on QVC rather than in Saks or Bloomingdales. I want women to be able to afford my clothes and not go into debt. You can afford to buy a little more and not break the bank.

And, of course, work toward the goal of a special purchase. Every woman deserves a nice pair of diamond stud earrings, a decent watch, and a gorgeous handbag.

We should be able to partake in that rich pleasure of buying something new — as often as possible within our financial means.

Mindfulness expert and psychotherapist Donald Altman has a cool trick to keep us in balance when it comes to shopping for the things we want — and, let's be honest — need! He writes in a column on the Mindful.org website:

"When you are shopping, take a moment and let yourself look with 'fresh eyes' at the abundance and variety that is before you. Ask yourself: Are the eye-catching colors helping me make a choice or is it filling me with fear that my usual choice isn't good enough? If you are going to purchase some fresh food notice the variety — not only in types but in color, the shape and packaging that is before you. Then ask yourself: Is the variety filling me with a sense of appreciation for the abundance that has graced my life or is it filling me with fear that the food I choose won't be quite right or I might need more?"

To me, these are words to live by. Women with Control should be masters over their environments, whether on the job, in the shopping mall, or in front of their kitchen pantry. When you choose to be more mindful while seeking out pleasures in life, you become more self-aware and more appreciative of all of the gifts in your life and in all that life has to offer.

CHAPTER 12

Find Their Passion

What are your favorite hobbies? I despise that question. The truth is, I don't really have things that I call hobbies. I'd rather not engage in "activities done regularly in one's leisure time for pleasure."

Hobbies? Non, merci. Not for me!

I'd much rather spend my time on **passions**. Honey, if I've got a little free time, why not spend it well? On things that really, truly excite me? My passions challenge me, intrigue me, and motivate me to be a better person. They make me WORK, but they don't feel like the work I do for my business. But just like my career, my passions are an important piece of my identity. They give my life meaning and help me feel like I'm fully engaged in the world. And, yes, they are a vital element to being a Woman with Control. The icing on the cake.

My Top 3 Passions:

Passion #1: My Grandkids. Aya and Levi are the two people in the world I will reschedule everything for, so I won't miss a birthday party or any other landmark event in their young lives. As a mother, I couldn't believe the amount of love I had for my son, but even that doesn't compare to the pure, utter delight that I get from spending time with my child's children. If you're a grandmother or "nene" (as I'm called), you get what I mean. If you're not, I hope you get to experience this level of love for yourself one day.

Passion #2: My Support of Public Theater and Parks. My father always said, "If you have a dollar, give a quarter." I'm passionate about the charitable causes I support. I support public theater, especially the Delacorte Theater in New York's Central Park. I love going to Shakespeare in the Park in the summer and look forward to taking Aya now that she's old enough. I'm a firm believer in "pay it forward," and I feel it's vital to support the public spaces and programs that provide for all.

Passion #3: Cooking. As you know by now, I relish entertaining. I love to host neighbors for summer barbeques and make home-made chicken soup with matzo balls for the Jewish holidays with my husband and the rest of the family. I use only the highest-quality ingredients: fresh herbs and edible flowers from my garden, organic vegetables, prime-cut steaks. I'm also a firm believer in buying locally sourced products. I try to frequent the farmers markets near my country house in Pennsylvania or in New York's Union Square.

We all need a reason to feel like we were put on this earth, and it has to be more than the careers we choose for ourselves. We need to strive for deeper meaning in life. And honestly, we need to have FUN!

As we near the end of this book, you should by now have picked up on a certain pattern. Every facet that defines a Woman with Control comes with a host of mental health benefits. You feel more empowered when you take smart risks. You feel a boost in self-esteem when you look in the mirror and see your best self because you've mastered your makeup and outfit. Well, the pursuit of passions may give you the biggest bang for your buck. A sense of fulfillment and the serenity that comes with it.

PASSIONS = INCREASED HAPPINESS

Robert Vallerand, a professor of psychology from the University of Quebec, found in his research that pursuing your passions leads to an increase in psychological well-being. He points out in a 2012 research article that to truly thrive in life, it's not enough to have a lack of stress. (Not to get morbid, but dead people have no stress.)

"Having a passion for an activity represents an important type of high involvement in activities that may lead to sustainable positive effects on psychological well-being," Vallerand writes. "Indeed, because people who have a passion for a given activity typically engage in this activity several hours each week, they may be experiencing positive affective experiences that should facilitate well-being."

Pursuing your passions also adds up to having more positive experiences in life. And we all need more of those!

Another bonus: Pursuing passions begets meaningful relationships because the people who share our passions are often those that we're more likely to connect with on a deeper and more rewarding level.

Justin (right) with grandchildren Aya (left) and Levi (middle)

I want you to do a quick exercise. Make a list of things you did today. Grocery shopping, exercise class, lunch with a friend, phone call with your daughter, meeting with architect to go over house renovation plans, etc. Put a plus sign next to all of the things you enjoyed. Put a minus sign next to all the things that were boring or downright unenjoyable.

Do your plus signs outnumber your minus signs?

Barbara Fredrickson, a psychology professor at the University of North Carolina, has documented that we need a 3:1 ratio of positive to negative events to stay in a state of well-being. Yep, the garbage in your life is far more powerful than the good stuff, so you need a lot more good stuff to bury the bad.

That's where passions come in. They're like a grand slam that takes it out of the ball park and gives you four runs, instead of the base hit you get from a pleasurable TV show.

Passions keep your positivity spigot flowing. They provide the deepest sense of happiness — gratification and, ultimately, a sense of gratitude that you're alive and healthy enough to appreciate the notes in a fine wine or a free play in Central Park.

For Wardrobe Warrior Tae MacKenzie, the ability to find and pursue her passions literally pulled her back from the brink. A successful runway model at age 26, she almost gave up on life after a severe stroke left her permanently disabled and in need of a wheelchair for mobility. "I was in a coma for three days, and when I woke up, my life had just stopped," recalls Tae, now 35. "I believed I wasn't beautiful anymore and that I had become invisible. Friends stopped calling. I lost my career. I thought about taking pills and ending it all."

Flipping through television channels one day, Tae landed

on QVC and Women with Control happened to be on. "Renee was the cutest thing doing her No More Wiggle, No More Jiggle dance. I felt like she was my auntie giving me inspiration," Tae recalls. "I just kept watching and feeling like I'd made a new friend. Renee was having so much fun with fashion that I thought maybe I could too. She was telling me it's okay to be a little different. Every woman is truly beautiful."

On a lark, Tae bought a pair of Women with Control pedal pushers and an Attitudes by Renee maxi dress, and she was amazed at how good her body looked in them. She started shopping more online, mixing designer brands with trendy accessories, and she found a friendly photographer near her North Carolina home for a photo shoot.

Before her session, she threw caution to the wind and put on heels. Killer stilettos. "It took me time to train my feet and get accustomed to wearing heels," she says. "My friends told me I was crazy, but I felt sexier."

She looked downright gorgeous, and she dangled a Louis Vuitton Carryall bag from the arm rest. The photos provided her with the proof she needed. She was still the same beautiful woman she'd always been, even if her life had been drastically altered.

Tae MacKenzie, Wardrobe Warrior

Tae had put her beauty back in the spotlight, and made women everywhere realize that they, too, could be sexy and beautiful, regardless of whether they were in a wheelchair.

"My passion is about what I can accomplish for the disabled community," she explains. "We need to be seen and admired for who we are."

More than 10,000 Instagram followers later, Tae is a star.

Check out her Instagram page:

instagram.com/tae_mckenzie/?hl=en

She rolls the runway during NY fashion week and her goal is to land a major TV role, like a medical resident on Gray's Anatomy.

"Women in wheelchairs exist and thrive," Tae says. "We have full lives and loves, and the world needs to know that. I thank Renee for bringing a piece of me back and helping me find my passion."

HOW TO DISCOVER YOUR PASSION

I can't tell you what you should feel passionate about. I'm sure your list looks quite different than mine. Each person has their own unique fire burning within, and you need to determine what makes yours burn brighter and hotter. Maybe you already know what your passion is, and that's terrific.

If you have no clue what gets your fire burning, Psychology Today suggests you follow these five steps.

1. Inventory your talents. "If God gives you something you can do, why in God's name wouldn't you do it?" — author Stephen King

2. Notice when you lose track of time, or what you hate to stop doing. "All the time I'm not writing, I feel like a criminal. It's horrible to feel felonious every second of the day. It's much more relaxing actually to write." —writer Fran Lebowitz

3. See your passion hunt as a fun, joyful adventure. "If I were not a physicist, I would probably be a musician. I often think in music. I live my daydreams in music. I see my life in terms of music." — Albert Einstein, whose passion was playing the violin

4. Think of what you loved to do as a child. "Love your calling with passion. It is the meaning of your life." — Auguste Rodin, who starting drawing at age 10 before turning to sculpture

5. Pay attention to what makes you [...] scared we are of a work or calling, the more su[...] that we have to do it." — screenwriter Steven Pressfield

I'm lucky because I have had the opportunity to enjoy my passions including my biggest passion of all — my career. I truly love what I do, and I love inspiring women like you to look and feel their best. My biggest risk in life was to leave that high-end job in fashion for a dream job that allowed me total control over my business.

Renee and Justin (middle) with grandson Levi (left)

I don't fool myself, though, into thinking that I have total control over my life. NONE of us has that kind of control.

...bout living life WITH control.

..., but we can make the most of

...ou look good and you feel good,

... you've got that inner fire burn-

...quer anything. Every grandmother,

...preneur, and young woman start-

ing out in the world ... ...ld find her passion and go out and nurture that dream. We all deserve to give ourselves that chance, and the world deserves to benefit from our unique contribution to it. I've gone through a lot in my life, and I've never let it deter me from doing what I want to do. I believe you can do this, too, even if you're not already working toward this goal. Thank you for joining me on this journey. Now go out there and make it happen!

Women with Control Team

STYLE IS NOT ABOUT SIZE - IT'S ABOUT ATTITUDE®

RENEE GREENSTEIN left college her freshman year and headed to New York City to pursue a career in fashion where she quickly became a fit model. During this time, she became aware that fashion catered to only a portion of women. She discovered her innate ability to communicate to designers and patternmakers how clothes fit and give suggestions on how clothing could be better made to fit all women. Renee's realization that STLYE IS NOT ABOUT SIZE, IT'S ABOUT

ATTITUDE™ inspired her to create her own clothing collections named Attitudes by Renee® and Women with Control ®. A line designed to be Inclusive of all sizes and empower all women to look and feel as beautiful as they are. Renee's collections are sold exclusively on QVC Global.

Hard work, determination, and never taking no for an answer has brought Renee to the point in her life that she wants to share the wisdom she has learned, the mistakes she's learned from, and the joy of doing what you love.

She has affectionately named her customers her Wardrobe Warriors™ and enjoys being able to speak with them through the means of social media, educating women on style, business, and sharing her philosophy of life. Renee is aware that the woman she designs for is a Multitasking Warrior™, and keeps this in mind when creating her collections.

When she is not busy designing or traveling the globe seeking inspiration, Renee is either in the kitchen whipping up one of her signature meals to entertain her beloved friends and family or spending quality time with her husband Justin, her son Corey, her daughter-in-law Jessica, and her two beautiful grandchildren, Aya and Levi.

By reading this book, Renee hopes you will gain the tools to dress for success and feel like a real woman with control… because after all Life is not a dress rehearsal, live for today!

→ Leopard Shoes

→ Magnetic eye Lashes

=

Made in the USA
Middletown, DE
05 July 2021

43631635R00118